Winter Camping

2d Edition

Camping

Stephen Gorman

APPALACHIAN MOUNTAIN CLUB BOOKS
BOSTON, MASSACHUSETTS

Cover Photograph: Rob Bossi
All photographs by the author unless otherwise noted
Cover Design: Elisabeth Leydon Brady
Book Design: Carol Bast Tyler

Distributed by The Globe Pequot Press, Inc., Old Saybrook, CT

Library of Congress Cataloging-in-Publication Data
Gorman, Stephen.
AMC guide to winter camping / Stephen Gorman.
p.   cm.
Includes bibliographical references (p.) and index.
ISBN 1-878239-83-X (alk.paper)
1. Snow camping. 2. Snow camping—Equipment and supplies. 3. Hiking.
4. Hiking—Equipment and supplies. I. Title.
GV198.9.G66   1999
796.54—dc21   99–44910
                                               CIP

The paper used in this publication meets the minimum requirements
of the American National Standard for Information Sciences—
Permanence of Paper for Printed Library Materials, ANSI Z39.48-
1984.∞

Due to changes in conditions,
use of the information in this book
is at the sole risk of the user.

Printed on recycled paper using soy-based inks.
Printed in the United States of America.

10 9 8 7 6 5 4 3   03

Contents

Acknowledgments v
Preface vi
Introduction vii

1. PLANNING 1

2. GROUPS AND LEADERSHIP 8

3. BEFORE YOU GO 16

4. GEAR FOR CAMPING 24

5. GEAR FOR WEARING 53

6. GEAR FOR TRAVEL 64

7. FOOD AND NUTRITION 84

8. ON TRAIL 94

9. BACKCOUNTRY SKI TECHNIQUE 112

10. ROCK AND ICE 133

11. IN CAMP 151

12. COLD INJURIES 172

13. FAMILY CAMPING 180

Afterword 191
Appendices 192
About the Author 196
About the Appalachian Mountain Club 197
Index 198

Traveling. . . like this is perpetual romance for me. This stump right here, this birch, this snowed-up brook; no, it is not these; it is on and on and forever on through the bright white wilderness and the shadowed trees. And best of all is to stand on a ridge and look ahead over infinities of nameless solitary country dreaming in the short winter sun. . . . Something keeps calling, on and on to the farthest ridges that lean against the sky.

—Elliott Merrick
True North

Acknowledgments

· ·

SPECIAL THANKS to my family and friends for all the good times we've shared on winter trails from Maine to Alaska, and everywhere in between.

Preface

● ● ● ● ● ● ● ● ● ● ● ●

I AWOKE IN THE DARK to the sound of wind rushing through the pass. The tent shook and the fly snapped. But as I lay still in my sleeping bag, I could hear something else—the whisper of falling snowflakes brushing the fabric of the tent.

Quietly I pulled on my boots and parka, taking care not to wake my companions, and stepped into the swirling storm. The snow was coming down hard. It filled the snowshoe tracks from the night before, wiped away all trace of last night's fire. As the birches and balsams shook and the snow whipped the air, I enjoyed a peaceful, almost euphoric, moment until I could stand it no longer:

"HEY YOU GUYS, WAKE UP! IT'S SNOWING!"

Just for good measure, I pelted the tent with snowballs, then dashed to the trees for kindling and firewood.

This is winter camping: the splendid forest scenery, the grace of falling snow, the companionship of friends. These have a way of making you feel like a kid again. Who doesn't have cherished memories of being snowed in—the unexpected gift of a day away from work or school? Who isn't gripped by a sense of adventure when snow forces a change of plan?

Winter camping is like being snowed in—it's being free from schedules and demands. It's an opportunity to be self-reliant: to feel the deep satisfaction of a snug shelter or a warm fire. It's a chance to slow down, renew old friendships, and enjoy life again.

And winter camping is a chance to play—to slide down a steep slope on the tails of your snowshoes, landing in a snowy pile at the bottom, to dig snow caves and to build igloos, to bombard your friends with snowballs, to have fun.

And fun is what winter camping is really all about.

As the Native Americans and Eskimos of the Far North demonstrate, life in the cold need not be all hardship and danger. Winter can be the favorite season, the bug-free season, the time when frozen lakes, rivers, and snow-filled forests make perfect highways for fast and easy travel. It is the time when animals can be located more easily, the time when the land seems strangely empty and silent.

It is also the time when the snow provides a slippery surface to send skis and sleds swiftly on their way, when the land is magically transformed from the drab grays and browns of late fall to the sparkling blues and crisp whites of winter. Living indoor lives, shielded from the elements by our computer-age technology, warmed by fossil fuels and nuclear power, many of us now see winter as the enemy, something to be gotten through. We shake our heads in wonder at people who spend time outdoors in the cold and snow. We have forgotten the pleasures of winter outings.

This book is dedicated to helping you discover the pleasures of snow camping and deals mostly with the fundamentals. It is designed to take you through the steps of planning, organizing, and conducting a trip on your own. It is for all those who wish to explore the winter wilderness, and experience the joys of winter travel, in warmth, comfort, and safety.

Introduction

HIDDEN UNDER THE SNOWY FOREST CANOPY, locked beneath the ice of freshwater lakes, and tucked away in the hollows of fallen trees, life in winter goes on. Though the land looks still, the residents are going about their business. After all, here in the North winter lasts half the year or more. Natural processes can't afford to hang fire for six or eight months. There's too much to do.

All life in cold environments prepares carefully for the onset of winter. Essentially, animals use one of three strategies for wintering: migration, hibernation, or adaptation.

Animals that migrate survive winter by fleeing to warmer climates. By escaping winter they avoid its rigors altogether, but they pay a hefty price in terms of energy consumed, and success is not guaranteed. Precious energy reserves may be depleted before the animal reaches its hoped-for destination.

Though migration as a wintering strategy appeals to many people, and mass human migrations occur every fall and spring, the cost is too high for most, and migration simply is not an option for everyone.

Some animals find a snug shelter, enter a state of reduced activity while maintaining their body temperatures above freezing, and hibernate. But because the animal must find a den where the temperature doesn't drop much below freezing, and the chance of finding such a safe haven diminishes the farther north one goes, hibernation as a strategy is rare among northern animals.

Hibernation is not a strategic option for people, though many endure a self-imposed imprisonment during the cold season, growing daily more lethargic and suffering from cabin fever.

Since avoiding winter through migration and hibernation just doesn't work for most northern animals, people included, the alternative is to adapt. Adapting means staying active and alert and coping with the seasonal changes in the physical environment. Wolves and caribou, fox and snowshoe hare act out their ancient relationships through the long arctic winter. And people, too, adapt, wintering successfully when they adjust to the season rather than fight it. Those who refuse, who instead try to impose an artificial life-style of perpetual summer upon the winter environment, face chronic discontent when the snow flies and the temperature drops.

The Athapaskan and Algonquian Indians of North America's interior forests and the Eskimos of the arctic regions perfected winter living and travel techniques over 10,000 years. For them, the winter environment is home. They have devised clothing, shelter, and methods of travel most appropriate for the cold months.

In winter the land looks still, but in the woods and waters life goes on. (Elk Range, CO).

Northern peoples have always found an ally in winter. The season makes their lives easier, not harder. Northern natives depend upon winter; they do not exist despite it. Winter makes life in the North possible and is the determining factor in how people live and travel.

For the hunter, mobility is of paramount importance. The ability to cover vast areas in search of elusive and widely dispersed game animals is critical to survival. Snow provides that mobility. Cold, hard, wind-packed snow is a surface enabling hunters in the barrens to cover a hundred or more miles in a day by dog-team. Snowmobiles, of course, need snow to cover equal if not greater distances.

In the interior forests, the frozen surfaces of an endless maze of lakes and rivers serve as a natural highway. Deep snow in the forest buries thick tangles of brush that hamper travel in summer. Speed and ease of travel is greatly enhanced by the onset of cold weather, and this increased efficiency is crucial to those who provide for themselves.

Europeans, particularly the French, were quick to adopt the native technologies for their winter travel in the North American wilderness. French fur trappers and traders recognized the importance of living among the native peoples, earning their trust and learning their ways, as the best method of doing business. Among the French to be a "Voyageur," a member of the great fur-trading brigades that traveled up-country among the Native Americans, was to be among the elite. To be a "Hivernant"—one who spent the winter in the field—was to have earned the highest distinction of all.

Today, it is perhaps harder than ever for outsiders to understand these relationships to the changing seasons. As we rely less on our own skills, less on predictable seasonal patterns, and as we alter our environment to serve us, direct contact with our surroundings becomes seemingly less important or beneficial. Modern culture insists you can't be comfortable when removed from the amenities of the latest technology, that living outdoors means roughing it—and who needs it rough? Not George W. Sears, a self-described "Old Woodsman," who in the 1920s wrote under the pseudonym "Nessmuk."

On the subject of roughing it Nessmuk writes: "I dislike the phrase. We do not go to [the woods] to rough it. We go to smooth it. We get it rough enough at home; in towns and cities; in shops,

Traditional hunting and traveling methods such as the dogsled require a good snowpack. (Maine Woods)

offices, stores, banks. . . . Don't rough it; make it as smooth, as restful and pleasurable as you can."

The best way to smooth out the rough spots, to be assured of a safe and comfortable winter experience, is to develop a sound set of skills. Skills give you the edge in your wilderness travels. With well-developed skills, you move through the country efficiently and with little impact, taking advantage of what your surroundings have to offer. You learn to avoid hazards and develop the confidence to handle critical situations. There is simply no substitute for skill.

Anthropologists, ethnographers, native elders, and others decry the fact that modern industrial society and its technology are rapidly replacing the traditional skills of indigenous peoples. They worry that healthy, viable cultures are being obliterated, that soon very little of the traditional methods and ways of life and the relationships to the earth that they imply will be lost forever. But indigenous peoples are not the only ones whose skills are vanishing, whose relationships with the natural world are suffering.

develop the right stuff

When learning, remember to move at your own pace. Expand your zone of comfort, but don't step out of it. A solid base of skills will stand you in good stead. If a trip is too ambitious for you now, don't worry; if you stick to it you will be ready some-day. The important thing is to have the right attitude. The experiences of two explorers illustrate the point.

The first, Sir John Franklin, was a likable, bumbling gen-tleman explorer commissioned by the British Admiralty in 1845 to discover the Northwest Passage through the Canadian Arctic. He was also a member of that school of imperial offi-cers who were steadfast in their contempt for the environ-ment and for native travel techniques. They clung to their notions of proper conduct, preferring (incredibly) to carry silver place settings and crystal decanters instead of food and supplies as they stumbled over the frozen arctic land-scape and slowly starved to death; the last survivors resort-ing in the end to cannibalism before they too expired. "Roughing it" indeed!

John Rae was a contemporary of Franklin's but of a dif-ferent breed. A tireless traveler in the service of the Hudson Bay Company, he would journey upwards of 1,000 miles over the course of a winter, often covering more than 25 miles per

There are still people, native and non-native, who are expert in the skills of wilderness living. Being an expert need not be a func-tion of your job, nor perhaps of how much time you spend in the field. A person can make the same mistakes year after year—I know people who do. As writer and outdoorsman Cliff Jacobson says, "Experts are distinguished by the style in which they travel, not by the difficulty of the trip, the frequency of those trips, or the number of days out." Style and skill are synonymous.

A high skill level is the result of patience, understanding, and respect—the essential energies put into a carefully nurtured relation-ship. By paying attention, by not imposing, we can hear what the day on snowshoes in one of the harshest climates on earth. Rae had no qualms about adopting native techniques. He made a study of Native American and Eskimo skills, his "heretical notion," as one historian puts it, being "that northern travellers should harness the ... environment to their advantage instead of struggling against it."

Predictably, the Admiralty disagreed, suggesting "The objective of. . . explorations is to explore properly and not to evade the hazards of the game through the vulgar sub-terfuge of going native." It was better to rough it as emis-saries of a magnificent civilization than to smooth it through the adoption of indigenous methods.

Ironically, it was John Rae who in 1854 discovered the ghastly truth concerning the final days of the Franklin expe-dition. Rae's report shocked the world with its horrifying revelations concerning the wretched demise of the expedi-tion's last survivors and earned him the everlasting hatred of the Admiralty and the British geographical establishment.

The lesson of Franklin and Rae is clear. Once we embrace the outdoors as our home—however temporary—we can begin to enjoy a closer, more intimate relationship with the land. The more we know about our environment, the more we try to understand the wilderness, the more pleas-urable, and indeed safer, our winter outings become.

land is saying. The dry snap of a twig teaches about kindling; the hollow sound of thin ice warns of danger; wind informs us of a com-ing storm; the calm silence of a snow cave speaks of sanctuary while the furies howl outside. Returning to winter, even for a few days, allows us to renew our relationship with the land and with ourselves. By listening, by paying attention, we can rediscover the fulfillment of coming home again and understand what Quebec poet Gilles Vigneault meant when he said, "My country is not a country, it is the winter."

1.
Planning
· · · · · · · · · · · · · · · · · · ·

EXPERIENCING THE UNEXPECTED—a great view or campsite, a foot of new powder on the downhill run—is one of the best parts of backcountry travel. If you plan well, you'll probably enjoy several of these "unforeseen" pleasures on your trip. But, if you are casual about planning and shortcut the process, you are far more likely to experience an unexpected disappointment, as happened to me not too long ago.

The snowy surface of New Hampshire's Umbagog Lake stretched like a white tabletop toward Canada. Under a gorgeous blue sky, our two dogsleds moved briskly over the smooth surface. We were making great time, conditions were right, everything was going according to plan.

We turned the dogs to the east, planning to intersect a trail marked clearly on our topographic maps. The trail, shown as a series of dashes coursing through an unbroken area of green, went overland through the trees.

But there were no trees. We climbed a steep hill, passed through a veneer of conifers, and emerged into a desolate wasteland stretching as far as we could see. Here, where the map indicated forest, was a massive clear-cut—industrial blight on an enormous scale.

Our maps had not shown the clear-cut. The lesson was clear: gathering as much information as possible before you set out is critical to the success of your trip.

WHERE TO GO

One of the big differences between winter and summer camping is that in winter, the backcountry expands. The crowds of summer are gone, and the carrying capacity of the landscape is no longer stretched beyond a sensible level. A popular summer hiking area reverts to a near wilderness when the snow falls. In winter, a rare encounter with another group of campers is not an intrusion, as it is in summer, but a welcome chance to share a moment with new friends. It's as if the winter wilderness were larger, more remote, more pristine. Wherever you go, close to home or far away, you are bound to discover new delights.

The first step is to decide on an area. Using guidebooks, road maps, or an atlas, you can pick an area of the country—or the world— that you want to visit. Now is the time to think big if you want a true wilderness adventure; or think small if you want a more personal, intimate experience. Get yourself psyched up. Cut out pictures of the area and tape them to the refrigerator. Talk about it with your friends or whoever will listen. Read the accounts of those who have been there. Project yourself into the landscape, savor the daydreams on your way to work.

There may be great winter camping right outside your doorstep. You can save time, gas, and money by not traveling long distances. A favorite local hiking area can be a great place for winter camping. Becoming familiar with a small wilderness may be as satisfying to you as trekking across a vast, expansive tract. Think about what you want to do. Do you want to do an easy, relaxing trip or do you want to challenge yourself and push your limits? You may want to mix it up a bit, blending relaxation and challenge into your own personal recipe for adventure.

Next, while you are still riding the crest of enthusiasm, gather more information. Make a list of people to contact—state, provincial, and federal land management agencies, local hiking clubs, and specialty shop owners and employees. When you've pumped them dry, ask where you can find out more. Write people who have traveled where you are going. Ask them about routes, local conditions, the best time of year to go, and other pertinent information. Be sure to include a self-addressed stamped envelope if contacting someone in the United States or include International Reply Coupons (available from the Postal Service) when corresponding with someone in

Organizing gear before heading out on the trail. (Kenai Mts., AK)

Canada. (Canadians should of course use domestic postage within Canada and IRC's when corresponding with someone in the United States.)

Simultaneously, start acquiring maps of the area. All maps—road maps, government maps, even tourist maps—contain useful information. And don't overlook maps put out by small publishing houses or local companies. They may contain up-to-date information missing from the official maps, especially where changes in land use have occurred. You can get local maps at local outfitter shops. See Appendix 3 for where to get U.S. government and Canadian maps.

Once you have gathered as much information as you can, make a base map. Take the government topographic maps and draw in all the new information that you have rounded up from other sources. Draw in new logging roads, buildings, or other land use changes. Note all the hazards or special sights people have told you about.

Pencil in your route, and check off every mile. Mark elevation gains and losses, and remember that climbing almost always takes longer in winter than in summer, whereas descending may be quicker. Note any physical features, such as open water, blown-down timber, or other obstacles that might cause delay. Try to find out what kind of weather and snow conditions you can reasonably expect. Then determine the distance you plan to cover each day of travel. Finally, look at your route and mark sheltered areas you can resort to in case of bad weather or injury. For each day of your trip decide upon the quickest and safest way out in the event of an emergency, and mark these escape routes on your base map.

HOW FAR?

How far should you plan to travel? That depends upon a number of factors, such as the steepness or ruggedness of the terrain, the weight of your pack, your means of travel, the pace of your slowest companion, the amount of time you can allot for your trip, and the time of year.

If the snow is either slush or deep powder, expect tough going. If the snow has settled, or the surface is firm and wind packed, traveling will be much faster. In the mountains, covering five miles may make for an exhausting day. In a valley, on a plateau, or skiing across a lake or river, you may be able to cover five miles in a couple of hours.

Check the map. If the contour lines are close together—indicating steep or rugged terrain—plan in the five- to ten-miles-a-day range. If the going is flat and wind packed, you may be able to knock off ten to fifteen miles or more per day.

There are no simple rules of thumb concerning distance. If in doubt, estimate conservatively. If you exceed your expectations, you can always take interesting side tours or enjoy a layover day. Some groups take a short trip into the wilderness to set up a base camp, then go on exciting day tours that are well within the group's capabilities.

WHEN TO GO

Late winter is an ideal time for your first trip or for a mountain trip. In temperate latitudes, the temperatures have moderated by late February or early March, the days are longer, and the accumulated snows of winter are piled high. Also, animals respond to the increased light and warmth. Your chances of seeing signs of wildlife activity are probably better. Give yourself a chance to get your skills down in a more benign environment before tackling a midseason trip with more extreme conditions. Just remember that the longer you wait, the greater the likelihood that you will run into rain and melting snow.

As you gain experience, you will time your trips to coincide with the cold periods, especially if you travel in areas where wide temperature fluctuations are common. Experienced travelers consider cold an ally. Early or late season lake and river ice can be dangerous, but hard midwinter ice is a fabulous travel surface. And subzero temperatures without strong winds are actually pleasant for traveling. In strong cold you are less likely to sweat while on the trail, easily maintaining a constant temperature with only a few layers on. Also, ice and snow conditions are good, and rain is extremely unlikely.

PLANNING FOR CONTINGENCIES

Be flexible, and realize that, no matter how well you plan, nature can make a mockery out of your best efforts. I once led an Outward Bound group that was determined to stick to its original itinerary, despite the fact that we were traversing a rugged mountain range that had received thirteen inches of snow on the second day of the trip.

By the fifth day the group was totally exhausted, having slogged only nine or ten miles in three days. They were frustrated and angry. They realized they would never reach their destination, and they certainly weren't having any fun. When my assistant and I suggested we consider getting off the ridge and descending to the gentle trails of the valley floor, they were stunned. Taking an alternative route had not occurred to them.

The next day, relieved of their burdensome goal, plunging down slopes through knee-deep drifts and skidding on their snowshoe tails, they had the time of their lives. The whole atmosphere of the trip changed.

Despite the best planning efforts, what is actually achievable depends upon local conditions at the time of your trip. Severe weather can move in and slow you down. Have a contingency plan prepared in advance. On your base map note all the sheltered areas where you can find protection in case of storm, and mark all the "bail out" points along your route. Knowing your alternatives in

Research and planning will help you find some of nature's wildest and loveliest winter destinations. (Chugach National Forest, AK)

advance will allow you to change your plan or retreat before you get into trouble. You will already know the quickest way to help in the event of an emergency.

PERMITS AND RESTRICTIONS

Notice the various land jurisdictions your route crosses. National, state, and provincial lands operate under different sets of regulations, and each may have a different mandate for use. A trip in the greater Yellowstone area, for example, may cross a patchwork of federal, state, municipal, private, and Native American lands. A trip in northern New England offers similar planning challenges, except that here the land is largely the property of timber corporations. A call to the government, or the company woodlands manager, will provide you with critical information.

Find out if there are any restrictions on winter travel in a specific area. Some parks, such as Maine's Baxter State Park, require that you apply in advance before you are admitted to the park in winter. Find out ahead of time, and you won't be surprised.

When you have arrived at your destination, check in with local authorities—National Park Service or Parks Canada rangers, state or provincial Department of Natural Resources officials, Forest Service personnel, and others who are in charge of local land and resource management. You can find them in the local phone book. Talk to people in town for up-to-the-minute tips on the area. Outfitters, guides, and specialty shop personnel are excellent sources of local knowledge. If you can, build in a day right at your jump-off point for gathering details concerning snow and ice conditions, weather forecasts, and trail information.

INTO THE UNKNOWN

In the past, some explorers traveled in regions for which no maps existed. They relied on their abilities and knowledge to pick up signals from the landscape and thus improve their chances of survival. Some traveled light: John Muir apparently set out on his journeys with only the barest essentials, having done only minimal planning. H.W. Tilman, a great British mountaineer, once remarked that if he couldn't plan a Himalayan expedition on the back of an envelope, it wasn't worth doing. Other explorers, such as the polar explorer Roald Amundsen, made extensive preparations before entering uncharted lands.

To these pioneers of yesteryear, the joys of unanticipated discovery outweighed the obvious dangers of entering the unknown. Their great experience and skill made their travels a calculated risk rather than a reckless gamble. The risk, though, was real. Some returned. Some did not.

The Appalachian Mountain Club does *not* believe that modern winter campers should try to emulate them. The equipment, maps, and travel techniques available today can make winter camping safe and enjoyable. The heroes of the past deserve their place in history, but the wise traveler of today seeks out as much information as possible before setting out into the winter wilderness.

2.
Groups and Leadership

GETTING STARTED IN WINTER CAMPING with a group is more fun and much safer than starting on your own. Group camping brings people together; the close interaction of a winter camping trip opens the way for mutual understanding and respect. Often, lasting bonds of friendship form between people who share the fun, laughter, and struggles of a winter wilderness experience.

The most important things to keep in mind when forming a group are goals, picking a team, group size, group skills, judgment, and leadership. The most effective groups consist of people who willingly contribute their own special skills and assets toward a common goal, thereby making the group stronger and more experienced than any of the individuals. The whole group thus contributes to each member's strength, confidence, and knowledge.

As long as the members work together, the group functions well. But group dynamics are volatile, and the literature of outdoor adventure is replete with stories of groups that disintegrated when goals became confused and personalities clashed. Even the most talented groups exist only as long as the individual members are willing to subordinate personal desires and work toward mutual goals. For any group to be successful, an agreed-upon mission, or goal, is essential. If misunderstanding or disagreement about the goals and objectives of the trip develop once it has begun, you are in for a rough time.

During the planning stage of your trip, call a meeting of all prospective group members. Everyone should express just what it is they hope to do on the trip. Goals may be different: one person may want to traverse a mountain range while another wants to make a base camp and take pictures. Now, rather than later, is the time to settle any concerns and to form a consensus.

PICKING A TEAM

Unquestionably, picking your teammates is the most important pre-trip decision. The wilderness has a way of bringing out a person's true character. If someone is selfish, moody, or short-tempered, the stresses of a camping trip will spotlight these flaws. Likewise, if your partners are responsible, cheerful, and fun to be with, these traits will be equally apparent.

If you can, travel with people you trust and know well. Many groups, once formed, take trips together year after year. Like a team on the playing field, they anticipate each other's reactions. They have learned how to work together and succeed.

Perhaps you know people you've enjoyed summer camping with. In any case, there must be a basis of trust. Decisions affecting people's safety must be made instantly, often on the basis of incomplete knowledge, by compatible group members. You cannot avoid the people you travel with day after day but must make every effort to get along as smoothly as possible.

My friend, Dan, once returned from an expedition where the group was highly incompatible: "We never really meshed as a group," he said. "So after the trip we did the next best thing. We split into six groups of one. After that, we got along fine—no hassles! Six different dinner reservations, six cabs to the airport. . . ."

What size group is best? Four might be the ideal number. In the event of an accident, one person can attend to the injured member while two go for help. Four is an easy number to cook for—a good-sized one-pot meal will amply serve four but may be on the skimpy side for five or six. Most freeze-dried foods come in packages of four servings as well.

Four people in one vehicle is probably the most cost-efficient way to travel. Getting more than four people and all their gear inside the average car (unless you have a van or a station wagon) is like trying to see how many people you can stuff inside a phone booth.

Six people can be a lot of fun, but groups of more than six lose the close, intimate feeling so desirable on a winter outing. With more than six, there are too many variables—more personalities, needs, desires, and abilities to contend with. The chances for incompatibility among the members increase as group size grows. Also, large groups may have a negative impact on the environment, exceeding the "carrying capacity" of an area, destroying the sense of solitude and space. In sum, the ideal group size is no fewer than four, no more than six.

Of course, the ideal is not always attainable, and you may have to scramble to find a third member when people back out at the last

A bond of trust is important—pick your teammates carefully and share the same goals for the trip. (White Mountains, NH)

minute. Don't cancel your trip; just be aware of the increased risks and take greater care to avoid problems.

One of the great advantages of traveling in groups is that each individual need not be expert at everything, as long as at least one person in the group has a necessary skill. One member may be a super skier, another highly skilled at ice travel. A third person may be a good outdoor cook, while a fourth is a genius with map and compass. By recruiting individuals with different strengths, the entire team gains in proficiency. The trip becomes more interesting if teammates can learn from each other and share their skills along the way. Just be sure that all the critical skills, such as first aid and navigation, are well represented.

LEADERS

Ninety percent of the decisions made during a trip will be arrived at democratically. There is no need for an autocrat to tell the group how far to travel each day, when to stop for lunch, or what to eat for dinner.

The group needs an experienced leader when there is disagreement over more serious matters, such as whether to cross a section of ice or bushwhack around, whether to travel on a stormy day or stay in camp, or how to proceed in the event of an emergency. The leader must always have the last word on decisions concerning questions of safety.

The leader is not necessarily the biggest, strongest, or most technically skilled member of the team, but he or she must be someone who is highly experienced and has demonstrated good judgment. The leader must have the confidence and support of all members and must not be afraid to make tough decisions for the group.

Whereas other group members may concentrate on their own experience, the leader focuses on the progress of the group as a whole, working diligently to insure the safety and satisfaction of the group. The leader, in short, must possess good judgment, must be self-contained, generous, able to call on reserves of extra energy, and have patience and understanding.

The best leaders—and the best teammates too—possess good judgment above all. Judgment is an intangible but essential quality that far outweighs any combination of specific technical skills. High-tech skills are desirable, of course, if you have set out to do a technically difficult trip. But proficiency is an asset only when it is guided by good judgment. Purely physical skills unguided by reason are like errant missiles—you don't know what damage is going to result.

Judgment means listening to your doubts and fears, not ignoring them. Judgment means knowing when it is safe to proceed, when it is prudent to retreat. Judgment is a calm levelheadedness that keeps you from straying too far outside your, or your group's, comfort zone.

Judgment results not only from experience but from careful attention to surroundings and events: the connection between a change in wind direction and a coming storm; fresh snow and unstable slopes; a hollow sound at the tap of a pole and thin ice. Some people are more receptive to these subtleties than others. These people make good trail partners. Seek them out. If you find them, stick with them. The leader, of course, is not the only one with a job to do. On expeditions people enjoy having responsibilities and like to receive recognition for what they do well. As part of your planning, the group should make a list of different responsibilities and divide them up so everyone has a job. Assigning planning tasks will give everyone a sense of commitment and also insure that everything gets done. Here are the planning jobs that need attention:

Researcher. The Researcher (often the Leader) gathers information concerning the details of the trip: when, where, and how far to go, permits, snow conditions, and other physical and regulatory details. The Researcher also compiles the base map and locates bailout options and contingency routes. He gathers a list of phone numbers—hospitals, state or provincial police, land management agencies—to use in the event of emergency. This list, plus a copy of the trip itinerary, should be left in the care of a Base Manager—a responsible person who is not going along on the trip.

Treasurer. The Treasurer handles the money. Every group needs a financial commitment from its members up front so that food, equipment, and other important purchases can be made, permits secured, transportation arranged, and so forth. The Treasurer estimates the costs of the trip, raises the funds from the group members, and acts as banker.

The Treasurer also needs to consider how to compensate nonmonetary contributions such as use of a member's car for transportation. Also, somebody always ends up lending out a lot of expensive equipment—such as stoves, tents, or sleds—which gets a lot of hard use. This use should likewise be factored in to the overall cost of the trip and the owners compensated.

In the interest of peace and harmony, all financial matters should be arranged equitably far in advance of the departure date, and the Treasurer should keep accurate records of all revenues and expenses.

Menu Planner. This person solicits meal ideas from the group members and creates a menu that is well suited to the physical rigors of a winter camping trip, is tasty, varied, and efficiently packaged. The Menu Planner, working with the Leader, also determines how much food is necessary for the trip. On expedition he or she keeps track of the food supplies and notes what is being consumed and at what rate.

Equipment Manager. There should be no chance that, two days into the trip, the group discovers that some vital piece of equipment was never acquired or was left behind. The Equipment Manager, in consultation with the Leader, generates a list of group and personal equipment, purchases the necessary items, and makes sure that everything makes it to the trailhead.

Naturalist/Historian. When someone learns about the human and natural history of the region, the trip takes on added interest. Knowing about the area you are passing through immeasurably enhances everyone's experience. The Naturalist/Historian may want to work with the Leader to incorporate sites of natural or historical significance into the trip itinerary.

Communications Director. During the planning process, one person must serve as the central information agency linking all the team members. The Communications Director makes sure that everyone is kept up-to-date on how planning is proceeding and makes sure that everyone knows what they need to be doing. The Communications Director can also serve as Photographer and/or Journalist. Group members and their friends will certainly be interested in the records from the trip, and local newspapers or magazines may be interested if you can document your experiences.

It should be clear by now that there is a lot of pretrip planning that goes into every successful winter camping trip. Depending upon your goals and objectives, this stage of the process can take a couple of months. The process can be as formal or informal as you like— some experienced groups that have worked together in the past know just what to do without much formal organization. In small groups one person wears many hats. The only thing that matters is that everything gets done before you head out the door.

When planning, start early, and give yourselves enough time to nail down all the details. As with other projects, details make all the difference. Once you have your base map, draw up a trip itinerary. For each day of travel write down your intended campsite, the number of miles to travel, bailout points, interesting natural or human-made features, hazards to watch for, if any, and any other pertinent information. Leave space to include the daily menu if you wish. Make a copy for everyone in the group.

GOING SOLO

The conventional wisdom is that you should never go alone in winter, period. But there are no absolutes in winter camping, and people do go alone, either by choice or by necessity. Most northern fur trappers work their lines alone all winter long, often spending a week or more on each circuit. Experienced travelers who feel sufficiently skilled and in possession of sound judgment sometimes elect to travel solo. There are no hard-and-fast rules, and traveling alone in the winter wilderness can be an intensely satisfying experience. However, it is important to understand the risks involved before you set out on your own.

The solo traveler is completely self-reliant. In the event of accident or injury, there is no one to help and little chance of rescue. Extra caution is required during even the simplest tasks because the margin of safety is so slim. An axe cut, an injury from a fall, a tent fire—should these incidents happen while traveling with others, the group can probably keep the situation from becoming desperate. But if they should happen to the solo traveler, the scenario becomes a grave one indeed.

When you travel solo, remember that everything takes much longer. No one shares the work, yet everything must still be done. Allow yourself plenty of time to perform camp chores, and since you will probably be breaking trail by yourself, be conservative in estimating daily traveling distances.

GROUP AND INDIVIDUAL SELF-RELIANCE

In our culture, wilderness is a place to get away from the impositions and complexities of modern society. In the wilderness we can enjoy an unusually high degree of personal freedom.

But, travel in the winter wilderness is not without risk. By its very nature, wilderness is beyond the power of human beings to control or pacify—and that's the way most backcountry travelers want it. But to enjoy it, each group member must do what they can to make the trip a safe one. Too often winter campers and mountaineers take the availability of rescue for granted. This laissez-faire attitude leads to relaxed planning, a false sense of security, and ultimately emergencies where the individuals or groups involved must be rescued, sometimes with tragic results. Implicit in accepting the freedoms of the wilderness is a willingness to be self-reliant—to accept responsibility for any situation that may arise.

When you plan your trip, do so with the assumption that your group will take care of an emergency by drawing on its own resources. Factor this assumption into your choice of partners, route, equipment, and contingency plans. Rescues are always expensive, they often expose rescuers to needless danger, and they generally result in a clamor to close the backcounty to winter travel. Those who would like to see the winter wilderness remain open and free should plan on being careful and as self-reliant as possible.

Don't push on if your senses are telling you to stop, and monitor the condition of the others in the group. Be honest with each other. If you are too tired to keep going, or have reservations about the wisdom of a particular plan, speak up. Be respectful of each other's opinions and feelings, and evaluate each situation as objectively as possible. Learn to distinguish between what you would like to accomplish and what is actually within the ability of the group.

3.
Before You Go

SO FAR SO GOOD. The hard part is over. You have put together a diverse and interesting group of people, chosen an exciting area to explore, gathered the information, and now you are finally ready to hit the trail! It's about time, you say. (We will discuss food and equipment in the next section.)

Well, you're almost there, but not quite. Remember, details are the difference between success and disappointment. There are a few things left to consider before you sling on your pack and head out into the winter wild.

First, you won't enjoy your trip if, after a mile of easy snowshoeing or skiing, you need to call the stretcher bearers. You don't need to be an Olympian to be a winter camper, but you do need to be in good shape. Not only will you enjoy the trip a whole lot more, you won't be a burden or a health risk to the group. If you exercise regularly you are probably in good enough shape for a winter camping trip. If you spend time in the outdoors on a year-round basis—hiking, canoeing, mountain biking, riding—being in excellent shape is a natural part of your life already, and you move with ease and grace from one season into the next. Urbanites who run, bike, go for vigorous walks, or play racquet sports at least three or four times per week will be physically prepared to get the most out of their trip. Those who are not used to regular exercise should begin a program well in advance of the departure date.

Staying active year-round will increase your enjoyment of winter travel. (Green Mountains, VT)

WINTERIZE YOUR VEHICLE

A group of weary, happy campers gets back to the trailhead at the end of a great trip only to discover that the cold has been playing havoc with their car while they were out playing in the snow. Before you go, make sure that your car is in shape for the trip, too.

Be sure to read the section on winter driving in your owner's manual, and give your car a basic tune-up before driving in the cold and snow. Check the following carefully:

Spark plugs. These should be in good shape. Replace them if necessary. Plugs are among the first parts to go in cold temperatures. And remember—if your car is fuel-injected, don't pump the gas pedal before you start it. You don't need to. If you do, you risk flooding the engine and fouling the plugs.

Battery. You want your battery at full power, so test it before you leave. Starting a cold battery at the end of a trip draws a lot of power all at once. If your battery is not in good shape, it may die at the trailhead and you will have push your car to jump start it.

Antifreeze. Be sure antifreeze is at full strength. People from the South should replace water with antifreeze before they head north.

Belts. Check the condition and tension of the belts. Bring spares if you are heading to a remote area.

Oil. Multiweight oils, such as lOW-40, are best because they are less viscous at low temperatures, making it easier for your engine to turn over in the cold. At super low temperatures, even multigrade oil may be too sluggish for your car to start. In this case, you may have to warm your oil pan. You can use your camp stove to do this in an emergency.

Gasoline. Cold temperatures can cause condensed water vapor to freeze inside your vehicle's fuel lines. There are two steps you can take to avoid this problem. First, leave your gas tank at half full or more. If the trailhead is a long drive from the last gas pump, bring along a full plastic gasoline jug and empty it into your vehicle's tank before you head out on the trail. Second, use dry gas. The alcohol solution in dry gas mixes with the water in your tank and keeps it from freezing. Small bottles of dry gas are available at almost every service station north of the Mason-Dixon line.

Washer fluid. It is truly amazing how much washer fluid you go through while driving to the trailhead. Slush and salty spray

Be sure your car is in shape for winter travel too! (Maine Woods)

thrown by other cars and trucks makes your ride hazardous. Be sure to top off your reservoir, and bring along an extra jug for the return trip. And while you are at it, check your wiper blades.

Tires. Snow tires are still the best bet where heavy snow conditions prevail. The deep tread of true snow tires bites into the snow and hangs on tight. If you plan on using snow tires, put them on all four wheels, and you will feel much more control.

All-season radials have replaced snow tires in all but the snowiest parts of the United States and Canada. All-season radials are better performers in wet and slushy conditions, and a set of four, especially with the designation M/S or M+S (for mud and snow), is probably the best solution for most winter conditions.

Before you put your trust in your tires, however, make sure they still have plenty of tread. A worn-down all-season tire will not keep you on the road. Remember, too, that low temperatures cause your tire pressure to drop-about one pound per square inch for every ten degrees Fahrenheit. Make sure they are inflated properly, and don't forget the spare.

Chains. There are areas where chains are mandatory on vehicles, especially in the high passes of the Sierras and the Rockies. A set of chains provides incredible traction. Check your owner's manual, and use them only as instructed. If you have never used them, practice at home before you set out.

Four-wheel drive. If you live in snow country, or often drive on unplowed logging roads to get to a winter trailhead, consider using a four-wheel-drive vehicle. Four-wheel drive is now available on many road cars as well as trucks and jeeps. Having all four wheels churning is a big help when you face a long drive through heavy snow, and it makes all the driving you do in winter conditions much safer.

In addition to winterizing your vehicle, be sure to have the following items in your car:

Car shovel. You will be bringing a shovel or two on your trip, and they are very handy to have along for the drive. If you end up in a snowbank, getting out will be a lot easier.

Scrapers. Bring two. You will always end up losing one.

Sack of sand and gravel. If you hit glaze or glare ice, you will have no traction. A small sack of sand can provide you with just enough grip to make it across these treacherous sections.

FINAL DETAILS

Before you leave, there are a few final details to consider:

Financial matters. Consider for a moment how you will cover the expenses incurred while on your trip, such as gas, tolls, shuttle fees, last minute equipment purchases, hotels, and meals. Once in the wilderness you will have no use for money, but what do you do with it before, during, and after your trip? You can carry cash, but you may feel vulnerable carrying large sums of money, and there will be opportunities for it to get lost or misplaced if you aren't careful.

By now everyone is familiar with the warning, "don't carry cash on your vacation—carry traveler's checks." Traveler's checks are safer than money. If you lose them you can get a refund but only if you save the serial numbers. Keep a record of the serial numbers at home as well as bringing them with you. Major credit cards are accepted just about everywhere these days, so they may be the best solution to the money problem. An added advantage for Americans of paying with credit cards in Canada is that you are billed at the actual rate of exchange, not at the reduced rate offered by most merchants. Still, as with cash and traveler's checks, if you lose your card it will be of no value to you.

Also, if you are an American going to Canada, the group's treasurer should be sure to convert your American money to Canadian currency at an American bank to insure that you receive the most favorable exchange rate. Canadians will find that some merchants in the northern states compete for their business and will take their money at par with American currency.

Vehicle shuttle. If you plan a long-distance linear route, you need to arrange transportation back to your point of origin, or you need to find someone to shuttle your vehicle to your final destination. In some national parks, or other popular camping areas, there are backpackers' and skiers' shuttles that will carry you and your equipment for a small fee. In more remote areas, call the local chamber of commerce. Often local guide or outfitting services will be happy to shuttle your vehicle for you. The fee is usually reasonable, and the time saved can be spent on your trip, not in the car.

Car keys. Be sure you know who has the car keys. On one trip we got to our final destination only to discover that the person who was supposed to have the keys had left them at our starting point.

The problem could have been easily avoided had we carried a spare set of keys, or if we had placed a set in a small magnetic box hidden somewhere under the car. If you have your vehicle shuttled, be sure both you and your driver understand where the keys will be left.

Personal trip journal. It always amazes me how many vivid details, memories, and feelings come rushing back when I reread a journal from one of my trips. A journal keeps your memories fresh when they would otherwise dissipate and blur with time. The extraordinary sights, activities, personal interactions, and insights you experience on a winter camping trip are worth preserving.

The journal need not be a chore. A typical entry can be as short as a few terse facts jotted in haste. Even these few details will trigger your memory of other events, bringing a flood of remembrances, helping you to re-create the sequence in detail.

Camera and film. Documenting your trip on film is one of the best ways to preserve the memories. A picture reveals at a glance what might otherwise take pages to describe. A carefully chosen sequence of images can tell the story of your trip, allowing you to relive it again with friends and family. Sponsors, newspapers, or magazines may have an interest in your photos if they are of sufficiently high quality and reveal important information.

Plan on shooting a lot of film. Even if you aren't a photographer, you will find that one roll of thirty-six exposures per day is not excessive. The images, enhanced by your written journal notes, will keep the trip fresh for years to come.

Equipment checks. Now is the time to be sure that all your equipment is in good shape and won't fail when you need it most. Be sure everyone has proper clothing, footwear, and sleeping gear. Check everything, making sure that rips are sewn, seams are waterproofed, screws are tightened, and bindings are adjusted. Be sure that the tents are in good repair and that no poles are missing. All the food should be purchased and packed, all group cooking gear accounted for.

Check the stoves. Start them and make sure they burn properly. Have everyone practice firing up the stoves before they have to operate them in the cold. Make sure that everyone understands the basics of stove repair. When tools malfunction in the cold, knowing how to fix them quickly is a highly desirable skill.

Check the weather forecast. Know in advance if it's going to be beautiful or if a major storm is going to pound you. You may choose to delay your start or make a contingency plan. Often heavy snow will not stop but only delay you. If so, adjust your schedule and let people know you may be a day or two later than anticipated. If you are traveling in avalanche country, you may decide on an alternate route. Check the five-day outlook for the area you'll be in.

Okay, by now you know that a winter camping trip consists of three parts-planning the trip, the trip itself, and learning from your successes and mistakes after the trip. But for now, the planning is over. Everything is ready to go. The team has been gathered, the car is packed, it's time to hit the road and get to the trailhead.

summary checklist:
planning

❅ Choose teammates

❅ Assign planning chores

❅ Pick an area to explore

❅ Locate sources of information

❅ Gather maps

❅ Make a base map

❅ Mark your route

❅ Pencil in critical information

❅ Plan for contingencies

❅ Obtain permits

❅ Winterize your vehicle

❅ Check the weather forecast

❅ Hit the road

4.
Gear for Camping

· ·

YOU DON'T NEED TO SPEND A FORTUNE outfitting yourself for winter camping. At least not if you don't want to. Marketing people are skilled at creating needs when all they are really doing is tapping into your desires. Be conservative when buying equipment. Buy the best quality item you can afford—you don't need an equipment failure halfway through your trip—and don't get something until you absolutely need it.

Much of the equipment you already use for backpacking, canoeing, and kayaking can be adapted to winter camping. For example, three-season tents are generally adequate if you stay off exposed ridges where fierce mountain winds blow. Large-capacity internal-frame packs are good for hauling loads in winter. Plan on using your backpacking stove, cook kit, and other essential gear and appropriate clothing on your winter journeys.

Borrow from friends, adapt what you already have, and if the item is not critical, make do without. This way, you can solve the cash-flow problem and live by Thoreau's timeless dictum: "Simplify, simplify, simplify." It's a lot less hassle, and you won't insulate yourself from your experience and your surroundings with piles of useless stuff. Remember that too much gear can be a trap, keeping you from ever becoming self-reliant and highly skilled. If you rely on high technology instead of your own know-how, you won't be able to handle the situation when your equipment fails.

The proper gear, used with skill, can extend your abilities beyond limits. So get what you need—the items that will help you become more proficient—and leave the rest behind. All that other stuff is going to end up in a landfill somewhere, and it will hold your skills development back.

Before you run out to the shop and get outfitted, there are a few questions you should ask yourself. Will you be skiing or snowshoeing? Do you want to travel fast and light through rugged terrain or take a more leisurely trip over easy trails? Are you headed into the subarctic, or will temperatures be a bit more moderate? Asking these questions now can help you sort through the equipment choices and make sure you get what you need. In this chapter we'll discuss equipment for camping and travel. Since clothing is a big subject, we'll deal with that in the next chapter.

Traditional winter camping gear and clothing. (Maine Woods)

PACKS

People have hauled loads on their backs since the beginning of time. The difference between then and now is that today's packs have sophisticated padding and suspension systems, allowing even the heaviest, most unwieldy load to ride comfortably on your back. For the winter camper, especially those who climb mountains or ski the hills and forest trails, the new pack designs have meant a welcome increase in freedom of movement and maneuverability.

An overnight pack for the winter backcountry must be big enough to carry your food, clothing, and equipment. The pack must be tough enough to withstand the stresses of bushwhacking and climbing; and it must be comfortable and stable, designed to allow you to move freely, unencumbered by awkward extensions or rigid attachments. Finally, the pack must have the necessary systems for securing skis, ice axes, and other winter equipment on the outside, easily accessible to the mittened hand.

There are three basic types of backpack: the external and internal frame packs for carrying big loads; and the day pack, a small, lightweight pack for day trips or side trips on longer journeys.

External frame packs. The classic big backpacks. These are the large, multicompartmented packs attached to a rigid outer frame. The rigid frame gives you excellent control of large, heavy loads by placing the weight high on your shoulders and in line with your spine, thereby putting most of the burden on your skeletal system and less on your muscles. The frame also holds the pack bag away from your back, allowing air to circulate freely, keeping your back cool and dry. And organizing your gear is simplified by the array of dividers in the pack bag and the outside pockets. For carrying heavy or awkward loads over moderate terrain, external frames are the right tool for the job.

The disadvantages of this type of pack for winter camping, however, are numerous. External packs reduce your freedom of movement and range of motion while climbing or skiing. The high center of gravity so advantageous while hiking can throw off your balance. Because external packs are off your back, they tend to sideslip when you rotate your torso, rather than rotate with you. In practice, this means that when you turn one way, your pack keeps going the other. The side pockets of external frame packs can also be a problem when you ski: while advantageous for organizing your pack, the side pockets restrict your ski poling—your arms tend to strike them on the backswing—and the tall frame can be a monster: it keeps you from being able to look up, can catch on branches when bushwhacking, and may bang you on the back of the head when you take a fall.

That said, many winter campers who know the pros and cons put up with the disadvantages in the interest of economy, preferring to use their summer external frame packs and avoid the added expense of buying a special winter pack.

Internal frame packs. These packs are much preferred by winter campers. Internal frame packs have stiff stays of metal, plastic, or synthetic fiber inserted into the fabric of the pack, providing a narrow internal frame that can be shaped to the contours of your back. Packed correctly, the load itself also provides stability. The advantages of internal frame packs for winter use are numerous. They give increased freedom of motion by holding the load

An internal-frame pack conforms closely to the body, increasing mobility and overall stability when you travel. (Teton Crest, WY)

close to your body, snugging it tight so that it conforms to your shape. This lets the pack turn and twist with you, making it much more maneuverable for skiing and climbing. The lower center of gravity keeps you well balanced on rough or uneven terrain. And the compact shape of the pack does not interfere with ski poling, nor does it get hung up in brush when bushwhacking.

One disadvantage of the internal frame pack is the care you must use when packing it. Because the pack is snug and formfitting, any haphazardly packed item will press against the back and annoy you. Another disadvantage is the lack of air circulating behind the back to keep you cool and dry (when it's really cold this can be an advantageous extra layer of insulation). With some packs you can add a foam pad to the lumbar region to make it more comfortable. Finally, the major disadvantage is the higher cost of the internal frame packs—while there are many good packs that cost less, top-of-the-line expedition packs can cost several hundred dollars.

Day packs. Day packs are handy to bring along for day hiking or touring once you have set up a base camp. They are usually large enough for extra clothing, lunch, a water bottle, first aid kit, and other accessories.

If you are going to be carrying home on your back for a while, make sure you have the features you need. A pack that doesn't have the capacity, doesn't fit properly, or is lacking in needed accessories can threaten your enjoyment of your trip. Here are a few features to look for when choosing a pack:

Size. Get a pack large enough to carry the additional bulk of winter gear, including fluffy jackets, hefty sleeping bags, food and fuel for several days, and so on. Of course, there seems to be an unwritten law of backpacking that requires you to fill any available space to the limit, but if you have a large pack, you will have ample room for everything you need for a multiday trip. A pack of around 5,000 cubic inches (different manufacturers measure capacity differently) or larger will do the job.

Suspension system. You'll be carrying most of the weight on your hips. Therefore, it makes sense to buy a pack with a comfortable, effective, and adjustable hip belt. Shoulder straps, which stabilize and support the load, keeping it close to your back and responsive to your motions, should likewise be easily adjustable,

A sturdy day pack can carry heavier loads, such as skis, when necessary. (Tuckerman Ravine, NH)

letting you move the pack away from or closer to your back as you wish. Make sure the packs you are looking at have a sternum strap, which helps keep the load stable and responsive to movement. All of these straps should be well padded. You should be able to adjust them while moving with your mittens on.

Compression side straps. These straps are sewn into the sides of the pack and are useful for compressing the load, keeping it from swaying or bouncing around. They also bring the load in snug to your back. You can also carry your skis and poles by sliding them through the compression straps alongside the main compartment of the pack.

Accessories. Some packs come with desirable extras, such as tabs for lashing on equipment; extending top pockets for increased pack capacity; removable top pockets that convert into large volume belt packs; ski holsters for securely carrying skis; lumbar pads contoured to fit into the small of your back; and torso pads to cushion your back against the load. All of these features can increase your packing options and make your life easier. However, they will also add measurably to the cost of the pack.

Fit. Before you take a pack into the winter wild, make sure you have the proper fit. Suspension systems are becoming so complex, we will soon need certified technicians to help us figure them out. Be sure to try the pack on in the store, under proper supervision, and fill it with the kind of heavy, bulky items you will bring on your trip. Simulate skiing, climbing, and snowshoeing motions. Ask the store personnel to adjust the suspension system. How does it feel? Is it comfortable enough for an extended winter camping trip? How does it compare to the other packs in the store?

Packs fit men and women differently because of their different body shapes. Men tend to have longer torsos, while women have longer legs. Make sure you get a pack that is designed for your body shape. Also, while fitting the pack, men should place heavy items higher in the pack, because their center of gravity is up near the chest; while women should place the heavier items lower, near their center of gravity in the abdominal area. Both men and women can carry heavier loads more comfortably if the weight is placed properly.

SLEDS

For years I adapted summer backpacking techniques to winter, traveling fast and light in the mountains unencumbered by lots of gear. But as the years passed I started taking longer, more ambitious trips deeper into the wilderness, and the backpacking paradigm no longer worked. In fact, for transporting loads on long journeys, canoeing is a better model. This lesson came home to me again recently on a multiday traverse of the Kenai Mountains in Alaska.

The Resurrection Trail wound through frosty subalpine forests and crested high, windblown passes far above treeline. Fortunately, we had done our homework and checked out the route in advance. The maps clearly showed a route that rose and then descended gradually over the course of forty miles.

So with no extreme ups or downs to hamper our mobility, there was no reason to carry backpacks. Instead we decided to use sleds on the traverse. The sleds allowed us to bring more gear and travel more comfortably than we ever could with packs, and for the next five days we traveled light and unencumbered, our sleds sliding steadily behind us. The mountain of food and gear that had seemed so imposing when spread out at the trailhead had vanished and was riding comfortably in a convoy of sleds.

Skiing with a sled is sometimes hard work, but compared to skiing with a heavy pack it can be blissfully easy. All the weight that you might have carried on your back is now sliding along behind you. Sleds are not the ideal solution in all types of terrain, but short of a team of huskies or a small army of porters, they do the job.

If you want to travel fast and light, you don't need a sled. Many winter campers prefer to go winter backpacking—adjusting their summer camping strategies to a winter environment. But if you want to take along the extras for added comfort or additional activity, if you want to set up a base camp from which to explore an area on day tours, or if you want to go deep into the wilderness on a lengthy expedition, then taking a sled is the way to go. With a sled you can carry your weight in food and equipment.

Here are some different types of sleds you may use:

Toboggan. For traveling over level or gentle terrain, a sledding toboggan is perfectly adequate. The sledding toboggan is essentially the recreational version of the sleds used for millennia by Native Americans in the northern forests. The Native American toboggan is

For heavier loads, use a sled. (Resurrection Pass, AK)

narrower, perhaps ten or twelve inches wide at the front tapering to six or eight inches wide at the rear. The tapering shape makes the toboggan track better.

The Native American toboggan is also quite a bit longer than the recreational sled (ten feet or more in length) and the front curl is curved higher, allowing the Native American toboggan to plow through deep drifts.

If you wish, you can take a knife to your recreational toboggan to trim the sides. The curl will not be as high as a Native American toboggan but will be adequate for most winter trips. The toboggan is easily hauled by attaching a loop of cord to the front at the base of the curl. Throw the loop over one shoulder and under the opposite arm and you are ready to pull.

Load your toboggan by placing the bulk of the weight slightly toward the rear to keep the front of the toboggan planing above the snow. Place a plastic tarp or a nylon or cotton tarpaulin on the toboggan, then load your food and equipment. Make sure no items are wider than the toboggan, or they will catch on branches, roots, and rocks. If an item is wider than it is tall, place it on end when you load it.

When the load is placed upon the toboggan, wrap it in the tarpaulin, or sled wrapper, and lash the load securely so that nothing spills out during the day. The sled should be able to turn over and not lose or shift the load.

Molded plastic sleds. For tours in more rolling or uneven terrain, it is advisable to have rigid bars connecting you to the sled so it doesn't run up on your heels during a descent. Also, runners on the bottom help the sled to track behind you, keeping the sled from zigzagging or sliding off a slanted trail. You can make your own sled or buy a commercially manufactured one. The molded plastic sleds available for a few dollars at toy stores can be adapted to winter trips. They are tough, have slightly raised runners that help keep them tracking, and are very inexpensive. A six-foot-long sled is big enough to haul food and gear for a substantial trip.

To adapt the toy-store sled to backcountry purposes, drill holes at spaced ten- or twelve-inch intervals all around the top of the sled sidewalls. Then, beginning at the front of the sled, thread a length of polypropylene rope through the holes along one side, around the

The Native American toboggan is an efficient tool for carrying gear to more remote spots. *Photo by Garrett Conover*

rear, and back to the front along the other side. The two ends of the rope, emerging at the front of the sled, are passed through (approximately) four-foot lengths of three-quarter-inch PVC pipe, which can be bought at any hardware store. The pipes should be long enough so that the sled stays well behind your ski tails on a descent or when you kick and glide on the flat. Then, tie loops in each end of the rope, clip a carabiner to each loop, and hitch the carabiners to the waist belt of a backpack or day pack loaded only with items you want to have handy during the day. Now, for a total investment of about fifteen dollars and thirty minutes, you are ready to go.

Load your sled the way you would load the toboggan, by putting the heavier items low and slightly toward the rear to keep the sled from tipping and to keep the front of the sled from nosing into the snow. Put a sled wrapper down first, then place all the items in the sled and wrap the load to keep snow and moisture out. Lash the load securely to the sled so that it does not come undone during the day.

Several of the commercial sleds are extremely well made—indestructible, lightweight—and come with a padded hip harness system that makes pulling them more efficient. The rigid harness and aluminum runners give you control that is impossible to match with the homemade sleds described above. Commercial sleds come with attached covers and lashing systems that hold the load securely and protect it from moisture.

SLEEPING BAGS

One of the most important equipment decisions Will Steger had to make while planning his 1986 dogsled expedition to the North Pole was choosing a sleeping bag. He needed a bag with plenty of thickness, or *loft*, to withstand minus seventy degrees Fahrenheit temperatures; with a well-designed *shape* to insure an efficient warmth-to-weight ratio; and with a compact *fill* material that wouldn't collapse when wet.

This last point is especially important, because during the eight hours or so that we are asleep, our bodies expel water vapor—approximately one pint of water per night. This moisture is *insensible perspiration* and occurs even when you aren't sweating but are merely at rest.

Insensible perspiration passes from the body into the fill of the sleeping bag, compromising its insulation value. Over the course of a multiday winter trip, a bag can accumulate this moisture and become saturated. In subfreezing temperatures, this means your bag will fill with ice if you don't take the time to dry it periodically. Pressed for time, Steger was unable to stop and dry out his bag. By the end of the eight-week expedition, his bag weighed well over fifty pounds.

What kept Steger (relatively) warm on his expedition was his decision to use a bag with fourteen inches of loft (the thicker the bag, the more ice could accumulate without total loss of warmth). His bag also had a tapered, body-contoured mummy shape to reduce heat loss and was filled with a synthetic fiber that packed compactly and retained some insulation value even when sheathed in ice.

The North Pole may not be in your travel itinerary, but if you plan on camping in winter, you face the same choices about loft, fill, and shape that Steger did when he was putting his outfit together. You need a good night's sleep after a long day on the winter trail, and your sleeping bag can be either a warm, pleasant haven or a frigid cocoon. A sleeping bag is your last resort in bitter cold. As with other equipment, it pays to shop wisely in the sleeping bag department.

Before you run out and buy a sleeping bag, ask yourself some important questions. As with most winter camping equipment, it is important for you to decide how you plan to use it. Keep the answers in mind as you shop for the winter bag that matches your needs.

Some winter campers are fanatical about weight. They'll do whatever they must to shave a few ounces from their pack, even if it means getting up a few hours early every morning to dry their lightweight down bags. Others, myself included, would rather put up with a little extra weight and sleep in.

Some people are cold sleepers, shivering through the night in a high-loft winter bag while friends are snoring soundly in an identical bag. Environment matters, too: some winter campers travel in cold, dry climates, while others can expect a snowstorm one day followed by freezing rain the next. Your choice of bag should take these factors into account. Here are some sleeping bag features to look for:

Loft. How warm a bag is depends upon the thickness of the fill. The thicker the fill, the more dead air spaces are created to trap warm air. Winter bags usually have eight to ten inches of loft, sometimes more.

Fills. Despite the development of new synthetics, goose down is still the warmest fill per given weight, providing about one-third more insulation than the same amount of any high-tech synthetic fiber. The result is an equally warm bag for one-third less weight. Down also compresses more compactly than synthetics, providing equal warmth for less bulk as well. For a warm, light, small bag, down can't be beat. Also, if well maintained, down bags can last twice as long as fiber- filled bags. So why not skip the rest of this chapter and rush out now for a down bag? There are other considerations.

Down absorbs moisture rapidly and the loft collapses when damp, rendering the bag into a useless sack of wet feathers. Remember, moisture comes not only from external sources—melting snow, sleet, rain—but from your own perspiration and respiration as well. On the trail you will literally be pouring a pint or more of water into your bag every night. Unless scrupulously dried on a daily basis, this moisture will quickly collapse your down bag, leaving you out in the cold. Vapor barriers stop perspiration wetting the down but can be uncomfortable.

Synthetic fills. Synthetic bags retain much of their insulation value when wet, making them top performers in cold, wet, and snowy conditions. They also dry quickly, and a synthetic bag can cost about half as much as a comparable down bag.

The main disadvantage of the synthetic bag is the extra bulk and weight you will have to carry—they can be up to 30 percent heavier and bulkier than comparable down bags.

If you choose a synthetic bag, you have three choices of fill material. Quallofil has the best warmth-to-weight ratio and compresses better than Hollofil and Polarguard®. But before you dash out and purchase the first Quallofil bag you see, remember that compressibility and stuffability depend upon bag design and construction as well, so shop around.

Shape. There is really no choice here: when winter camping, go with a mummy bag. Rectangular bags, although roomier, are much heavier and much colder. Mummy bags contour the body closely and thus are the most efficiently shaped sleeping bags, offering the most warmth. Mummy bags also have an insulated hood that can be

A sleeping bag will stay warm and comfortable if it is dried out in the morning prior to being packed. (Teton Crest, WY)

drawn closely around the head, keeping the warm air inside the bag from escaping.

Look for a mummy bag with a well-insulated draft tube that lies against the full length of the zipper to keep cold air out, and make sure the bag has an insulated collar that wraps around your neck to prevent the escape of warm air and the entrance of cold air.

Size. Make sure you get a bag that is comfortable but is neither too large nor too small—just big enough for you and your boots (placed in a stuff sack at the bottom of the bag). Your body must generate extra heat to warm up empty air space. If your bag is too small, however, your movement will be restricted by the contoured shape of the bag. A rule of thumb: if you plan on traveling in very cold areas, get a bag that is big enough for you to sleep in with your parka on and long enough for you to put your boots inside at the bottom of the bag.

Temperature ratings. These figures are useful but far from precise because there is no industrial standard rating system for comparing the bags of different manufacturers. You may find one bag rated at zero degrees Fahrenheit perfectly warm and shiver the night away in another bag with the same rating. For comparison within a certain manufacturer's line, however, these figures can be helpful.

Another problem with temperature ratings is that different people have different metabolic rates. The bag you are comfortable sleeping in at twenty degrees below zero Fahrenheit may be an icebox for someone else. What can you do? Be conservative in estimating how warm a bag you need. Experiment in a controlled setting, such as a back yard or a local campground. If you aren't sure, go with a warmer bag.

Instead of buying a winter bag, you can use a thin summer weight sleeping bag inside of a three-season bag. Make sure there is plenty of room for you and your boots. While perhaps a more economical solution, this system may add bulk and weight. Try this system before you head out on a long trip.

SLEEPING BAG ACCESSORIES

Sleeping bag covers. There are plenty of times when a sleeping bag cover comes in handy. These coverings of waterproof breathable fabric keep your bag from getting wet from melting snow inside snow caves, from spindrift if you are sleeping under a tarp, or from the snow that people invariably drag with them into a tent. If you are sleeping out under the stars or on a high mountain ledge somewhere without shelter, they are essential.

The extra layer of fabric not only keeps moisture from penetrating your bag from the outside, it keeps wind from stealing your warmth, and it creates another layer to trap warm air.

Sleeping bag covers are not trouble free. The moisture expelled by your body during the night passes through your sleeping bag insulation. Some of this condenses as frost when it reaches the outer layer of sleeping bag fabric and can be brushed off in the morning.

But with a sleeping bag cover, the moisture condenses as frost between your bag and the bag cover. Unless you are careful to brush it off every day, this frost can work its way back into your sleeping bag, increasing the amount of moisture already present there.

Vapor-barrier liners. These inner bag liners of nonbreathable material will keep your sleeping bag insulation dry by intercepting your insensible perspiration during the night, preventing it from passing from you through the fill material. A vapor-barrier liner can add measurably to the temperature rating of your sleeping bag.

The problem with vapor-barrier liners is the humid atmosphere they create inside the sleeping bag. I have always found them cool and clammy, prohibiting a good night's sleep. However, many people use them and apparently achieve excellent results. The best way to discover what works for you is to experiment by borrowing or renting one and using it in the back yard on a cold night.

Sleeping pads. Keep in mind that snow-covered ground is cold and that whatever insulation your bag provides for your back will be crushed by your weight as you sleep. The result? You may be warm on top, but that cold ground will suck the warmth right out of you, keeping you shivering all night long. What can you do? Put some insulation between your sleeping bag and the ground. The more the better. An easy way to do this is to use a sleeping pad. There are three basic types: open cell pads, closed cell pads, and air mattresses.

Open cell foam pads are comfortable if thick enough. Because open cell foam pads compress easily, they need to be at least one-and-one-half inches thick. Since these pads absorb moisture like a sponge, most open cell pads come with a cover.

Closed cell foam pads don't compress as easily, so you can go with a thinner (3/8 inch) pad. On very cold nights, however, you'll want more insulation, so carry two of these pads on midwinter trips. Closed cell pads aren't as comfortable as open cell pads, but they don't absorb moisture.

The typical air mattress is the most comfortable sleeping pad, but it quickly drains your body heat away because there is no insulation within the air chambers of the mattress. An answer to this problem is to carry an extra foam pad to use on top of the mattress or to use a mattress with open cell foam inside the air chamber, such as a Thermarest®. These combine the comfort of open cell foam, an air mattress, and a waterproof cover. You must be careful not to puncture an air mattress, so bring along a patch kit just in case.

Clothing and packs. Use your extra clothing and your pack to keep you off the cold ground. Putting your pack under your legs and feet adds insulation, while arranging a layer or two of wool or pile under your head and shoulders will also add to the efficiency of your sleeping pad.

TENTS

Fellow Maine guide and winter camper without peer Garrett Conover is not impressed with the new generation of high-tech tents. "Tiny superlight tents take on the look of sensory deprivation chambers," he says, "with the additional torture of possibly having to share such a space."

Exactly.

When Garrett goes into the winter woods, he takes along his ten- by-twelve-foot wall tent made of fine-weave Egyptian cotton, a lightweight sheet steel trail stove, and a pair of kerosene lanterns. The whole outfit weighs about forty-five pounds, but, Garrett says, no one has ever complained once they were basking in the sixty-five-degree Fahrenheit heat on a cold winter night.

Garrett packs his tent on a Cree toboggan, where it rides securely alongside his other equipment and provisions. With this outfit, even a severe cold snap—"bragging cold" as he calls it—is spent in warmth and luxury.

Where you go determines what you need (or can afford) to bring. If you aren't headed into the mountains, there is no reason to be Spartan. Leave the backpack behind, find a large tent with a collapsible wood-burning stove, and put it in the sled. On a cold winter night, you'll relish the warmth and extra space.

If traveling quickly or heading to the mountains is your plan, a truly lightweight shelter is what you need. Backpacking tents (not bicycle touring tents or "bivvy" shelters) are portable vacation homes. Just whip the tent out of the stuff sack, set it up, and there you are—home for the night.

Most backpacking tents consist of two layers: a waterproof fly that stretches over a breathable inner canopy. This two-layer system

Some winter campers prefer the traditional wall tent—not exactly lightweight, but with a stove it's luxuriously warm in any temperature. (Maine Woods) *Photo by Garrett Conover*

is designed to keep the inside of the tent dry. The fly prevents moisture from entering the tent from the outside, while water vapor from wet clothing, breathing, and perspiration passes from the inside of the tent through the breathable canopy to the outside.

If properly sealed and stretched close to the ground, the fly is effective at keeping moisture out. But moisture from the inside does not always pass through the breathable canopy. Instead, when the temperature inside the tent is warmer than outside (a desirable situation), moisture condenses on the cold fabric and collects as frost on the ceiling of the tent. When this happens, knocking the interior walls will trigger miniature blizzards—the price you pay for the additional twenty degrees Fahrenheit or so of warmth a tent provides. Tents come in various shapes, sizes, and colors. Domes and pyramids offer the best use of space, are wind stable, and resist snow loading well. They allow you to move around freely and sit face to face with your tent mates. Tents with an **A**-shaped frame, on the other hand, restrict your movement and force you to face front or back, never side to side. Also, the walls of **A**-frame tents always feel like they are hanging over your shoulder or in your face.

The best tents for winter camping are the four-season models. The walls of these tents are made of nylon panels that trap body heat; the floor is a high-sided waterproof "washtub" design to keep ground moisture from penetrating; the poles are made of extra strong aluminum (avoid fiberglass, which can shatter); and there are plenty of lash tabs sewn onto the fly for securing the tent in strong winds. A nice added feature is a removable vestibule for storing equipment under cover or for using a camp stove while snug in the comfort of your sleeping bag.

Make sure to get a tent that is large enough for comfort. With all the extra clothing and equipment of a winter outing, it helps to have extra space. I find that two people can live quite comfortably on a multiday trip in most three-person tents (for comparison purposes, the dimensions of The North Face VE-24, the classic three-person expedition tent, are: height: 49 inches; floor: 104 inches x 84 inches; area: 47.7 square feet). Of course, you can squeeze in another person if you must, but then it can become quite cozy. I prefer tent

Dome tents are stable, resisting both wind and snow loading well.

doors that open to the side. With doors that open to the front it is easier to track snow inside the tent. Also, I prefer the cross-ventilation and four-season versatility offered by a tent with a large no-see-um screened rear window rather than snow tunnels, which I find I never use in even the worst conditions.

Backpacking tents come in a full range of colors, and this can make a difference when you have been out on the trail for several days. The brightly colored tents filter the sunlight, adding a cheerful cast to the light inside the tent. Even when the day is overcast and gloomy, these bright colors have a way of creating a pleasing atmosphere.

STOVES

Even if you plan on doing your cooking over a fire, pack along a stove. On stormy days you can cook with your stove right outside the tent while you remain snug in your sleeping bag. In the event of an emergency, a stove can boil water in minutes, leaving you free to attend to other business. And by using a stove, you can lessen your impact on a heavily used area. In some places, stove-only policies have been implemented to protect fragile environments from decades of poor fire-building practices.

For a winter camping trip you will want a tough, reliable, easy-to-use stove that puts out a lot of heat, operates in cold temperatures, and is simple to repair in the field. For mountaineers, light weight is also a factor.

White-gas-burning stoves are best for winter use. *White gas* is additive-free automobile gasoline and is highly volatile. Some of these stoves sound like jet airliners and burn like blowtorches—you can practically rob a safe with them. White gas burns very hot even when it is extremely cold out, is easily obtained in North America, and is relatively inexpensive. Coleman fuel and Blazo are trade names for white gas and can be purchased at any camping supply or hardware store.

White gas stoves must be pumped occasionally to maintain pressure inside the fuel tank and require priming with preheat fuel—minor chores that tremendously increase performance and heat output.

The efficient, lightweight white gas stove is the best choice for winter.

Although many winter campers cook inside their tents on stoves, the practice cannot be recommended. Carbon monoxide is a by-product of white gas combustion—the noxious fumes have caused the demise of more than one arctic explorer—and preheating the stove sometimes causes a flare-up capable of reducing your tent to a puddle of melted toxic goo in seconds. Be careful.

Other fuels are available for camping, but few have as many advantages as white gas for the winter camper. *Unleaded automobile gasoline* is widely available and less expensive than white gas, but check first to see if your stove can use it without becoming clogged by the additives. If so, it may be the best choice for you. *Kerosene* burns hot, is inexpensive, and is widely available, and is safer to transport than regular gasolines, but it is hard to light, is smoky, has a strong smell, and takes a long time to evaporate if spilled. *Butane* works terribly in the cold, and you must pack out the nonrenewable disposable canisters. *Propane* burns well at subzero temperatures, but the bottles weigh two to three pounds apiece, a sufficient disincentive for most stove users. *Blended fuels*, a mixture of butane and 20 percent propane, work better than straight butane in cold weather, but you are still stuck with lugging nonrenewable disposable canisters. *Denatured alcohol* burns cool, producing about half the heat per weight of gasoline, is expensive, and stoves that burn it are hard to find. Alcohol is advantageous because it is safer than other fuels due to its low volatility, and it is not a petroleum product.

When operating a stove on the snow, you'll find it has a tendency to melt the snow underneath, causing pots to tip over. One ingenious friend has solved this problem by bringing along an old license plate, which he puts under the burner. The trick works. In any event, you will need to insulate the burner from the snow with something—a tin can lid or an extra pot top will also do the job.

A major deterrent to stove performance is wind. Many stoves come from the manufacturer with specially designed windscreens. If not, then placing the stove out of the wind during operation is also a good idea. Snow blocks can be arranged around the stove to block the wind as well. Carry your fuel in round, aluminum Sigg bottles specifically made for this purpose. The bottles are lightweight, unbreakable, and the lids are sealed with rubber gaskets to prevent them from leaking. Fill your stove through a small funnel with a screen for trapping the impurities that can clog your stove and impede its performance.

How much fuel should you bring? That depends upon how often you plan to use the stove, whether you need to melt snow for water, and how elaborate your meals are. A rule of thumb is to bring one-quarter to one-half cup of fuel per person per day. By keeping your stove well maintained, clean, shut off when not in use, and out of the wind, you can make a small amount of fuel go a long way.

COOKING UTENSILS

Two large nesting pots—one for the meal, the other for hot drinks— and a separate frying pan suffice for a group of four. Make sure that both pots have covers to keep the heat in and stray matter such as ashes or pine needles out. Pack the pots and pans in a stuff sack designated for the purpose. If the pots nest one inside the other, you will have an easier time packing and transporting them.

A pot grip (or a vise grip from the repair kit) is handy for grabbing pots and pans, and if you do a lot of cooking over a fire, a pair of leather fireplace gloves is very useful.

When you're sledding and can afford the extra weight, consider bringing a reflector oven for baking in front of the fire. If your group has a talented baker, treat yourselves to fresh-baked brownies, coffee cake, and muffins. Also, since cooking at high altitude takes much longer than at sea level, those of you out in the western states and provinces may want to pack along an aluminum pressure cooker to speed up cooking and rehydration of dried foods. A small grill or fire irons are useful for cooking with pots and pans over the fire or to keep food warm near the fire.

Complete your kitchen set with a ladle, a serving spoon, spatula, and, if you are feeling decadent, a small whisk for mixing ingredients. Toss in a scrub pad for cleanup.

For hot drinks I like my insulated mug with the top that clamps on and keeps the heat in. With these cups you must punch a hole in the cover and tie it to the handle or else you'll lose the top within a day or two.

For eating, bowls work best. You can use them for soups, stews, pastas, and other meals without worrying about the food spilling or getting cold. A bowl can do everything a plate can do and is much more practicable in the outdoors.

Plastic bowls work well, but they can melt when placed too near the fire and tend to absorb food odors and colors. If you use them for chopping, your knife will leave cut marks that fill with grime and little live organisms. Enamel bowls are a better choice because they don't hold odors and can be used for chopping and slicing. Also, enamel can double as a pot lid or a container for boiling water if necessary.

What else do you need? To get the food to your mouth use a spoon. A spoon can do just about everything a fork can do (except perhaps skewer your ziti) and is more appropriate for most of the hooshes (an explorer's term meaning any one-pot meal—traditional hooshes were concoctions flavored with seal meat) you will be eating. You can get plastic spoons that don't conduct heat at outdoor shops, or you can forgo the luxury and bring one from home. Since spoons are easily lost, it pays to be careful, bring an extra, or tie a loop to it and wear it around your neck.

REPAIR KIT

You may not be able to count on great snow conditions or finding the perfect campsite, but you can count on your equipment breaking or wearing out. What do you do when a binding screw backs out? Limp back to the car? Never! Just dig into your repair kit, find a replacement, and ratchet it into place with your palm-sized posidrive screwdriver.

Lots of things can go wrong with your gear on a winter camping trip, but just about everything can be fixed with a simple repair kit. Here's what you need to bring along:

Sewing kit. A couple of heavy-duty needles and a spool of heavy-duty thread or a packet of dental floss will take care of most rips in your clothing or equipment. For really tough material, bring along a small awl or hole punch—a feature on most Swiss Army knives. Which leads us to:

Swiss Army knife. These little self-contained toolboxes come in handy a hundred times during a trip. From cutting nylon cord to slicing cheese, it's an invaluable piece of equipment. The basic model I use has two blades, an awl, a Phillips head screwdriver, a bottle opener with a regular screwdriver head, and a can opener with another, smaller screwdriver head.

Nylon cord. If you need to make a splint or a stretcher, if you need a clothesline or want to lash something onto your pack, if you need a new bootlace or need to lash a broken snowshoe frame, you can do it with nylon cord. Bring fifty feet or so.

Phillips head screwdriver. A #3 Phillips head fits cross-country ski bindings. Many specialty shops sell small posi-drive models.

Extra screws. Bring extra binding screws. Oversized screws can hold a binding in place if the original screw hole has been stripped. An assortment of screws of different sizes for general repairs is useful.

Pole patch kit. If your pole breaks you can fix it by splinting it with a pair of curved-backed snow tent stakes and duct tape. Similarly, aluminum flashing or sheet metal and hose clamps will do the job. Bring along an extra pole basket too.

Duct tape. Perhaps the most useful item in your repair kit. You can use it for fixing just about anything, from a broken pole or ski to splinting a snowshoe or patching a rip in your tent fly. The stuff is a miracle. I even wrap my heels with it to prevent blisters.

Spare stove parts. Bring along spare parts to fix your stove in case of breakdown.

Fire-starting kit. Have a waterproof container of matches and fire-starting material hidden away in your repair kit or somewhere dry. For fire starter, some people use solid fuel pellets or flammable liquid fire starter in tubes. I prefer to stash away a handful of dry birch bark for emergencies.

Spare bindings. If a binding breaks, it's a lot easier to put a new one on than try to improvise with nylon cord. A spare set of bindings for the group can save the day.

Vise grip. A small vise grip comes in handy as a clamp, for loosening tight parts, as pot grips, and for a dozen other uses.

Glue. Superglue can fix a stripped binding, broken glasses frames, and a hundred other things. Make sure to pack it carefully so it doesn't leak all over.

File and file card. A file keeps your ski edges and your axe blade sharp, the file card keeps the file clean and ready to use.

OTHER EQUIPMENT

Axe and saw. Axes and saws are controversial equipment items, but they are indispensable to some campers. With a saw and an axe you can provide enough firewood to keep a camp warm all night in a short time, even in wet weather—an important safety consideration. And on an extended tour it is impossible to dry wet clothing, equipment, or people without a source of heat.

Without a heat source you must rely on your body to generate warmth and your clothing to retain it. With a fire you have a powerful external heat source that can make your trip much more pleasant or can rewarm you in the event of serious trouble. On a cold night you need a fire or you must retire to the warm insulating folds of your sleeping bag as soon as you stop moving, missing out on the evening around the fire, one of the timeless reasons for taking to the winter woods in the first place.

The problem with fires in heavily used areas is obvious. Most people opposed to camp fires are rightly concerned with local environmental impact and suggest the use of stoves instead. Unfortunately, stoves do not provide adequate heat output to serve as drying or warming mechanisms, and they certainly do have an impact on the environment, though not necessarily a local one. As Garrett Conover points out, stoves have a displaced impact. "A stove user," he says, "has enlisted a global army of extractors, refiners, smelters, manufacturers, and distributors, all of whom deal with nonrenewable resources, contribute to toxic waste through manufacturing and transportation processes, and provide an end product that requires the use of finite

A saw and axe (with cover) are extremely useful when used wisely.

fuels once the stoves are in use. Stoves have their place, but like the automobile, they are not a low- impact piece of equipment."

Used wisely, a lightweight axe and folding saw can make clean and efficient use of a local renewable resource-wood-and provide you with many hours of pleasure and comfort as you bask in the warmth of a fire on a cold winter night.

Wax kit. If you are going to be skiing, and you don't have wax-less skis, you'll need a simple wax kit. Few backcountry skiers are concerned with performance waxing—the mixing and blending and secret incantations used by Nordic ski racers—but they are interested in adequate grip and glide. Many ski campers simply carry a cork, scraper, and the two-wax system.

The two-wax system is simple—one wax is for dry snow, the other for wet. The two canisters are color coded so you don't get confused, and that's about as complicated as it gets. Use the waxes sparingly at first. If you need more grip, apply more layers of wax and lengthen the wax area. The beauty of the two-wax system is that it handles a wide range of snow conditions and performs well in transition snow. The wet-snow wax does a good job providing grip on the uphills and won't ice up as readily as klister. It is also much easier to apply and to remove. For steep uphills, however, you may have to resort to klister or put on the climbing skins.

Other backcountry skiers take a full range of waxes, klisters, and wax removers. You will definitely get better performance when you fine-tune waxes to conditions, but balance out the desire for results with the realities of skiing with packs or sleds. A compromise plan used by most backcountry skiers is to bring a small selection of hard waxes, universal klister. climbing skins, and the two-wax system.

First aid kit. Naturally, every group that goes into the winter wilderness needs a first aid kit, and a suggested list of what it ought to contain is presented in appendix 2. Some items, such as sunscreen and lip balm, should be kept handy because they will receive a lot of use.

Group gear. Other group equipment includes a couple of shovels for digging fire pits, building snow shelters, constructing

Backcountry skiers try to keep waxing as simple as possible, sometimes adding a fresh layer of the two-wax system during a lunch break.

You will need a shovel and snow saw (with homemade case) if you plan to build snow shelters.

kitchen areas, and uncovering avalanche victims, if necessary. Grain scoops work well for most snow removal, but if you are going into avalanche country make sure your shovel has a strong, tempered aluminum blade for cutting through packed ice and snow quickly.

Snow saws are invaluable for building snow shelters and digging into wind slab or rain-hardened snow. The blades are lightweight yet sturdy aluminum with forward canted teeth for ripping through packed snow.

A small diameter rope is helpful for added protection and support when crossing streams or descending steep or icy pitches. One hundred twenty feet of 8MM Perlon rope is adequate for most situations where a safety rope is required.

Personal gear. Handy personal items include sunglasses for bright days and goggles for when the snow flies; a headlamp, which keeps your hands free and can be invaluable if you have to travel after dark; and an avalanche beacon and avalanche cord, which are a must when you travel in areas where slides are common. Ice axes and crampons are essential for anyone planning alpine routes; and of course, everyone should have a compass and know how to use it.

summary checklist: gear for camping

Personal Gear

- Pack—External or Internal Frame
- Day Pack
- Sleeping Bag
- Sleeping Pad
- Sleeping Bag Cover
- Vapor-Barrier Liner
- Compass
- Headlamp
- Wide-Mouthed Water Bottle
- Camera/Lenses/Film/ Extra Batteries
- Journal
- Reading Material

Group Gear

- Maps
- Towing Sleds or Tobog- gans
- Tents
- Tent Stove
- Cooking Stove
- Fuel Bottles
- Coleman Lantern
- Candle Lantern
- Axe
- Folding Camp Saw
- Snow Shovels
- Snow Saw
- Small-Diameter Rope (120' of 8MM Perlon)
- River Rescue Throw Rope
- Wax Kit
- First Aid Kit
- Cooking Equipment
  - 2 pots with lids
  - 1 frying pan
  - spatula
  - pot grips
  - fireplace glove(s)
  - reflector oven
  - pressure cooker
  - small grill or fire irons
  - metal tray or lid for fire building
  - small metal tray or license plate for cookstove
  - insulated mugs
  - bowls
  - spoons

5.
Gear for Wearing

"THIS IS ABOUT AS WILD AS IT GETS," I thought as I gave up the lead and let someone else break trail for a while. As he passed, Stu shouted something like "What a day!" I just shook my head. No use talking; the wind literally whipped the words right off your lips and cast them into the great beyond.

I fell in behind Stu, second in a line of five heading down an endless white wind tunnel of a lake in northern Maine. Soon I was mesmerized by the lift and step, lift and step of his snowshoes. Flying snow pellets struck my goggles like BB shot. The wind carved the snow into delicate, enchanting shapes—little mesas, canyons, and spires—each crystal catching the sunlight like the facet of a diamond.

At noon the temperature reached a high of about twenty degrees below zero Fahrenheit. The wind was gusting at forty to fifty miles per hour, hurtling across the lake like a semitruck screaming down a long grade. This deafening roar made communication impossible. We were isolated, next to but cut off from each other. But as long as we could keep moving briskly, as long as we had no equipment problems, as long as we didn't have to stop for very long, it was safe to keep going.

Because I was properly dressed, I was not conscious of being cold. I wore a few light insulating layers under my wind parka and wind pants—a layer of synthetic long underwear, light wool shirt, and wool pants—and was thus able to stay comfortably warm while moving and keep the wind out. On my head I wore a thin synthetic balaclava, a hat, face mask, goggles, and my parka hood. My feet were snug inside a layering of liner socks, vapor-barrier socks, two pairs of medium-weight wool socks, and mukluks. My hands were cocooned inside a warm layering of liner gloves, heavy wool mittens, and windproof mitten shells. Not an inch of skin was exposed.

The layering worked. Each of us stayed warm and dry. We had gauged the weather and our efforts correctly. The wind was kept out and just enough body heat kept in to keep us comfortable. That night, in camp after all the work was done and the temperature plummeted to new depths, out came the heavy insulating layers.

Away from the fire, out on the lake at thirty-five degrees below zero Fahrenheit, I watched the stars dance in the frigid sky. I heard the trees crack and pop in the cold and listened to the lake ice boom as it contracted and shifted. Bundled up in all my layers, I felt like Neil Armstrong on the moon, but I was warm.

The key to putting a winter camping wardrobe together is to make an assessment of the weather conditions, determine your activities, and dress accordingly. Knowing that you will be snowshoeing and pulling sleds all day, burning up some 4,000 or 5,000 calories, you sure won't need to look like the Michelin Man. The synthetic pile pullover, the heavy vest and parka, can stay in the sled. They can come out when you stop moving, when you need them to retain body heat with heavy insulation.

On the trail, the trick is to stay warm and comfortable without overheating. The light, loose layers allow you to release most of the body heat you generate. Yet these layers trap enough warm air to keep you comfortable while avoiding a dangerous sweat, which not only robs body heat but reduces the insulation value of clothing by up to 90 percent. The windproof garments keep the wind from stealing too much precious warmth, yet are loose enough to allow excess heat to escape.

LAYERING

When winter camping, wearing the right clothing combination will add to your enjoyment and performance. The key to your comfort is the layer system.

Clothing does not provide you with heat; your body does that. Rather, clothing provides insulation to keep your body heat trapped, much as a thermos bottle provides insulation to keep a drink warm. Clothing insulates by trapping air between fabric fibers or layers of clothing. These "dead air" spaces hold air that has been warmed by your own body heat. The more dead air space you provide, the warmer you will be. This is why several layers of clothing are warmer than one thick layer.

Your layers must be dry in order to be effective. Water fills and collapses dead air space, rendering the garments virtually useless. However, there are materials that perform better than others when damp. Wool retains some dead air space when wet, allowing you to retain some heat. Synthetic fabrics such as pile, polypropylene, and others are very effective at heat retention when wet. Cotton, by contrast, unless treated or woven very finely, absorbs water and actually causes you to lose body heat through conduction.

A layering system can be broken down into three categories: inner layers, insulation layers, and outer layers.

Inner layers. These are worn next to the skin. Inner layers provide some insulation and transfer moisture away from your skin,

Wearing the right clothing in three layers—inner, insulation, and outer—will keep you warm and dry. (Southern NH)

keeping you both warm and dry. Wool or synthetic long underwear such as polypropylene, a thin balaclava, and liner socks and gloves comprise this layer.

Insulation layers. These middle layers provide lots of dead air space that traps and retains body heat to keep you warm. Wool or synthetic pile shirts and pants, a synthetic jacket or wool sweater, and a synthetic or wool hat and mittens are the standard garments. In the evening you can add a heavily insulated down or synthetic parka with hood to wear over the other layers.

Outer layers. These act as a barrier to prevent wind and rain from stealing your warmth. Outer layers keep your body heat in and inclement weather out. Mitten shells, a face mask, and a windproof anorak or parka and pants of nylon, or a water- proof/breathable fabric do the job. Be sure the jacket has a hood.

The layer system allows you to adjust your insulation as you heat up or cool down. Remember, you are the one providing the warmth, not your clothing. So when you are snowshoeing or skiing and start to warm up, shed a layer. If still too hot, take off another. Then, when you stop for lunch and are no longer cranking out the BTUs, put all those layers back on before you cool down, and trap a reservoir of warm air.

Each layer performs a specific, unique function. No one layer can do it all, but when you coordinate the different layers and use them properly, you discover how they complement each other. The result is a flexible system that can be adjusted instantly according to your need and preference.

That's the beauty of the layer system. Now let's take a look at the various clothing components, from head to toe.

CLOTHING COMPONENTS

Head. The old saying about putting on a hat if your feet are cold holds true. Some 70 percent of your body heat can be lost above your shoulders. So keep your head covered, and don't neglect your neck. To reduce heat loss from the head and neck area, the best protection is a balaclava. These headpieces cover everything from your topknot to your shoulder blades, while leaving an opening for your nose, eyes, and mouth.

Wear sunglasses to protect your eyes.

You'll also want to bring along a hat, maybe two. At least one of these should be a thick, warm wool or synthetic pile hat that will keep you warm on cold days. Wear your hat over a thin balaclava and you will be comfortable even on bitterly cold days. The other hat can be a lightweight beret, wool cap, or a baseball cap for days when it is too warm for a heavy-duty hat.

If you anticipate crossing exposed areas, such as mountain ridges or frozen lakes where the windchill can be severe, bring along a face mask. If exposed on extremely cold and windy days your nose and cheeks can freeze within a minute or so. On such days, ski goggles should be worn over the mask, covering every inch of your skin from the chilling blasts.

Layering goes for your head, too—a balaclava, hat, hood, and goggles help keep heat in and chill out.

Upper body. Keeping your core warm will go a long way toward keeping your whole body comfortable. As with your head, if your torso is well insulated, your body can afford to send blood out to your extremities and keep them warm, too.

Your inner layer of long underwear should be wool or a synthetic such as polypropylene. Both materials do an excellent job of keeping your skin dry by wicking moisture away. Most winter campers choose the synthetics over wool because they believe it wicks better, dries faster, and is more comfortable. I have used an angora wool blend on my most recent trips, however, and find it similar to the synthetics in terms of performance and equally, if not more, comfortable to wear.

For insulation up top, bring several layers. A lightweight wool or synthetic shirt will be fine for most days, but a synthetic pile jacket will be a real pleasure to throw on when you take a break or travel on really cold days. Like wool, synthetic pile retains warmth when wet. Pile is also lightweight, very comfortable, and dries out quickly. A nice feature of pile is its warm, cozy feel.

Bring a heavy down or synthetic fiberfill parka for cold nights. It should have a heavily insulated hood. In very cold weather you can bundle up in the parka and stand around the fire looking like the Goodyear blimp. So be it. The more you add to your girth, the warmer you'll be. As for materials, down is lightweight and easily compressed but loses loft when wet. Synthetic parkas are bulkier, heavier, but retain warmth when wet and dry quickly.

Your outer layers must keep the elements out, so it is a good idea to have a waterproof shell. Here you run into the problem of

Make sure your parka has an insulated hood.

perspiration again, however. If your shell garment doesn't breathe, then the moisture produced by your body will be trapped between layers.

Waterproof/breathable shells help transfer moisture to the outside, are reasonably waterproof, and are excellent at cutting the wind. But there is no way that any garment is capable of letting all of your perspiration pass through if you are working hard. Even with a waterproof/breathable shell you will become damp from your own perspiration if you don't pace yourself and ventilate properly. Rather than count on miracle fibers to do the impossible, you might do well to save your money and look at less expensive shells.

If you choose to use a less expensive waterproof shell, be sure to wear fewer layers underneath, and ventilate it properly by keeping zippers open, sleeves open at the cuffs, and leaving it loose at the waist. Slow your pace, or stop and cool down. To retain warmth, do just the opposite. Cinch your garment at the waist and move briskly. Slow down and ventilate before you begin to sweat.

There are garments that feature zippers for ventilation, and these help dissipate heat and moisture. Remember, however, that the more your shell is perforated with openings, the less waterproof it will be in a downpour.

Lower body. Layering applies to your legs as well. Start with a layer of long underwear. Then, on a warm day when you are active, wear a pair of shell pants over this layer and be on your way. On a cold day, or in camp, add a pair of wool or pile pants. The beauty of pile pants is that many come with side zippers for ease of putting on or taking off over your boots. Wool pants without side zips are much less versatile as a layering component.

For your lower legs, gaiters are a must because they keep deep snow from entering your boot tops. Most winter campers choose knee-length gaiters. A good pair of gaiters has a Velcro® flap covering the zipper to keep it from icing up. Mukluks users won't need to worry about gaiters because the uppers reach to just below the knee.

Feet. Your feet are without doubt the toughest part of your body to keep warm and dry. They are farthest from the heat source, and they are always in contact with the cold snow. Not only that, but they produce lots of perspiration while you ski or snowshoe, making it extra hard to keep them warm.

Keeping your boots and socks dry is a real problem. Moisture from the snow permeates your boots. While you can use snow seal on your boots to keep moisture out, the snow seal will block the transfer of moisture from your feet to the outside air. If you don't block moisture from your feet right at the source, you will thoroughly soak your socks and boots from the inside. What can you do?

Fortunately, there is an answer. For feet, combining the layer system with the vapor-barrier system works best. Wear a thin liner sock of wool or polypropylene next to the foot. Over this wear a vapor-barrier sock—a coated nylon sock or thick plastic bag—to trap the moisture generated by your foot. Over the vapor-barrier sock wear two medium-weight wool or synthetic socks. With the vapor-barrier sock trapping foot perspiration, your insulating socks and the inside of your boot will stay dry. Putting a plastic bag over your insulating socks will further protect them from moisture permeating through from the outside of your boot. You can also use foot powder or rub your feet with antiperspirant to cut down on moisture.

A final touch to prevent your boots from becoming wet is to use a randed gaiter. The rubber rand seals the boot, preventing moisture from working through to soak the leather.

When you get to camp, change your damp socks for dry ones, and exchange your heavy ski boots for a pair of cozy down or fiberfill booties. Put a felt insole inside for extra warmth. Then, pull a pair

Shell pants and mukluks keep your lower body warm.

Hand layers should be flexible, warm, and easy to put on and take off.

of canvas or pack cloth mukluks over these booties to keep them dry as you set up camp, and enjoy the evening in warmth and comfort.

Hands. Layering for your hands begins with a pair of thin liner gloves made of silk, wool, or polypropylene. Liner gloves are sometimes all you need to wear on warm days or days when you are working hard and there is no wind. They keep your hands warm and dry while permitting the manual dexterity to perform such tasks as using a camera, waxing a ski, putting up a tent, or lighting a stove.

Wool or pile gloves can be worn over the liner gloves for more warmth on cold days. On very cold days, wear a pair of heavy wool or pile mittens. Cover these with mitten shells to keep wind and water out. As a last resort for cold hands, or if you constantly need to remove your hands from your mittens on cold days, use chemical heat packs inside your mittens. They put out lots of heat and last for hours.

CLOTHING FEATURES

Size. Your parka and shell gear will have to be able to fit over a lot of bulky items. Make sure you get them a size or two larger than your regular size. The best way to be sure when purchasing a shell is to try one on over all the layers you plan on wearing on your trip.

Other clothing items should fit loosely and comfortably. Tight clothing restricts your freedom of movement and reduces the amount of dead air space available between the layers.

Seams. If the garment is designed to keep water out, make sure the seams are properly sealed. Most camping supply stores sell tubes of seam sealer. Check the stitching on other seams. If it is loose or worn, fix it before you head out the door.

Snaps. Avoid pieces of clothing that close only with snaps. They fill with ice and snow and either will not close or else they freeze shut. If you have items with snaps, replace the snaps or the garments or avoid using them for winter camping. Zippers with Velcro® draft flaps are preferable.

Zippers. Every zipper on every piece of clothing or equipment should have a zipper pull—a piece of fabric or string—so you can grab hold of the zipper with your mittens on. Having to take your mittens off every time you need to adjust an article of clothing is a good way to get frosted hands.

Pockets. Choose a shell garment with a couple of large pockets. You will constantly be using them for various and sundry items, such as matches or lighters, snacks, maps, compasses, etc. Hand-warmer pockets are great too. Just remember the trade-off—the more features your shell has, the more opportunities there are for water to work its way in.

summary checklist: gear for wearing

Head
* Synthetic balaclava
* Synthetic or wool hat
* Face mask
* Goggles

Upper Body
* Synthetic or wool long underwear
* Lightweight synthetic or wool shirt
* Synthetic pile jacket
* Down vest
* Down or synthetic fiberfill parka
* Waterproof/windproof shell

Lower Body
* Synthetic or wool long underwear
* Synthetic or wool pants
* Waterproof/windproof shell pants

Feet
* Synthetic or wool liner socks
* Vapor-barrier socks
* Synthetic or wool socks
* Ski boots or mukluks

Hands
* Synthetic or wool liner gloves
* Synthetic or wool gloves
* Synthetic or wool mittens
* Waterproof/windproof mitten shells

6.
Gear for Travel

SKI DESIGNS HAVE COME A LONG WAY since the thirteenth century when Norwegian King Sverre's Birkebeiner ("Birchleg" for the birch bark leggings they wore) scouts slipped through the snowy Scandinavian forest on eight- to twelve-foot-long hand-hewn boards. But it wasn't until the mid-1800s that Sondre Nordheim, a skier from the Telemark region of Norway, took a critical look at what the Birkebeiners were using and decided he could make a few improvements. By whittling a bit here and shaping a bit there, Nordheim created the first pair of what we might recognize as modern skis.

Then Nordheim went one step further. He attached twisted vines to the boards, wrapping them over his toes and around his heels, thus creating the first heel binding. Now Nordheim not only had (relatively) lightweight gear, but his new bindings allowed him to control his direction as he scampered over the landscape and down the slopes.

Soon, Nordheim and his fellow Telemarkers were dominating ski competitions throughout the country. The technique they used to steer their skis—dropping into a crouch, one ski forward, one ski back—became known as the "Telemark turn." Ever since, backcountry skiers have been imitating Nordheim and his merry men.

Leave it to another Norwegian to take Nordheim's invention and put it to use on an extended trip. In 1888 Fridtjof Nansen used skis on his daring crossing of the Greenland ice cap. Then, in 1911, yet another Norwegian, Roald Amundsen, used skis to become the first man at the South Pole. There was no longer any question about the usefulness of skis (by now called "Norwegian snowshoes") in the winter wilderness.

Before the first ski lift was installed in 1934 in Woodstock, Vermont, skis (and skiers) were equally adept at going uphill, going downhill—even jumping. But when lift-served skiing eliminated the need to climb, the sport became much more specialized. The backcountry skier, with his do-it-all equipment, was almost eclipsed by the flashy downhillers with their shiny outfits and locked-down heels.

Today, skiers are again taking to the backcountry on versatile yet ever more specialized equipment. The 1990s saw an explosion in backcountry and telemark gear, and picking the right pair of skis can be confusing. As with all your other winter camping equipment choices, it's important to ask yourself how you intend to use the skis. Will you be touring through moderate terrain, or will you be skiing extreme chutes and making first descents down 50 degree slopes? The answer to this question will steer you to the right pair of skis.

SKIS FOR THE BACKCOUNTRY

Touring Skis

For most winter camping trips that incorporate backcountry ski touring, journeys where the primary goal is to cover ground and not seek out steep hair-raising descents, backcountry touring skis are an excellent choice. The best backcountry touring skis incorporate lightness and are wide enough at tip and tail to provide stability and flotation in deep snow and narrow enough under the foot to provide sidecut for ease of turning. The width measurements of a backcountry touring ski (tip-waist-tail) are roughly 65-55-60MM.

Backcountry touring skis also have metal edges for control on icy or steep terrain and *camber*—an arch in the middle of the ski. The area underfoot created by camber is called the *wax pocket*. When the ski is weighted, the wax pocket compresses, coming into contact with the snow and giving the ski some grip. When weight is removed, the wax pocket lifts off the snow, permitting the ski to glide forward.

Leave the lift-serve crowds far behind with backcountry touring skis and bindings to help you. (Sierra Crest, CA)

Most backcountry touring skis are double-cambered, which means that even when you put your weight on the ski, you must still press down to flatten it against the snow. The advantage of double camber is that it holds wax better on a long trip and also provides some spring to your kicking and gliding.

Finally, the tips of a backcountry touring ski are stiff enough to provide a stable platform on hard-packed snow and ice but not so stiff that they cut into deep soft snow and disappear.

Telemark Skis

In the last decade, increasing numbers of backcountry skiers have headed into the high, wild country along the spine of North America's great mountain ranges. From the Appalachians to the Alaska Range, for tours involving steep descents in untamed territory, the new breed of ski mountaineer has opted for a wider, heavier ski that more closely resembles an alpine board than a backcountry touring ski. With measurements up to 99MM at the tip, the new telemark skis are virtually indistiguishable from alpine boards. In fact, many budget-minded backcountry skiers simply slap free-heel bindings on their old lift-served skis and head to the hills.

Wide telemark skis offer the winter camper heading to rugged terrain several hefty advantages. Their width provides a stable platform for a skier with a heavy pack, and their fat dimensions allow them to float in deep powder and bust through crud and heavy wet cement with ease.

Naturally, there are tradeoffs, and wide telemark skis do have some significant disadvantages. They are heavier than backcountry touring skis, so they will slow you down on long, flat tours. Their single camber construction means they won't add any spring to your stride. Finally, the lack of a wax pocket mean they must be used with climbing skins during virtually all ascents.

That said, for winter campers who hope to cut up some backcountry powder along the way, the advantages of wide telemark skis more than make up for any drawback. However, if you are more interested in general touring and have little desire to link turns on moderate to extreme steeps, then classic backcountry touring skis will serve you quite well.

The best place to learn about top-quality skis is through the buyer's guide of outdoor magazines followed by visits to a Nordic shop connected with a touring center or to an outdoors specialty shop. Make sure you get all the facts, and remember: it's always best to try before you buy. Many shops have demo skis for this purpose, and manufacturers often have demo days at ski areas and touring centers.

One of the most important questions you'll have to answer about skis is: waxable or waxless? Not all of us live in a blue-wax powder heaven (a skier's paradise), but if you do, this is a silly question. Would you ride a three-speed in the Tour de France? Of course not. If it's high performance in good conditions you want, go waxable. Waxable skis perform better than waxless skis. The waxables glide better, slide through a turn better, and work better on hardpacked snow and ice. With some knowledge of waxing, you can fine-tune your skis to the prevailing conditions. And waxing really isn't such an arcane science once you've done it a couple of times.

Waxing your skis actually heightens your awareness of the environment. You learn to differentiate between many types of snow and match them with the proper wax for high-performance skiing. A perfectly waxed ski is a joy to ride, qualitatively different from a waxless model.

Despite new design breakthroughs, the waxless ski that can keep up with the waxable ski has yet to be invented. The main difference is the ski bottom. The mechanical designs on the waxless

Transition snow can bog down a waxable ski. In these conditions, waxless skis come into their own. (Green Mountains, VT)

bases provide grip on the snow but also add friction and impede glide. No matter how sophisticated these designs, you can still hear the zippering sound many waxless skis make as the bases slide over the snow and slow the ski.

That said, waxless skis also have their place. They are great for changing, transitional snow conditions. One warm spring day I skied merrily by on a new pair of waxless skis as my friends bogged down on their waxables in transition snow. At lower elevations their klister wax worked well, but as we climbed, the slush turned to cold white powder. Soon, they had no glide at all—the snow clumped up on the bottom of their skis like platform soles and they were walking around like clowns. It took twenty minutes for them to get all that mess and goo off their skis and replace it with the proper wax. In sum, for performance in steady conditions, go waxable; for highly transitional conditions, go waxless. If you do most of your skiing in areas with variable weather or at the beginning or end of the season, the added investment in another pair of skis may be worth it to you.

SKI BOOTS

Be careful when shopping in the boot department. Make sure you get a boot that is comfortable, warm enough, and rugged enough for years of hard use. Boots are perhaps the single most expensive investment you will make as you put your skiing outfit together, and they'll also be one of the most important to your comfort.

Your boots are critical to your skiing. If warm and well constructed, the boots will allow you to ski comfortably and skillfully. If poorly fitting or not well made, they will be an expensive source of misery until replaced.

Leather Backcountry Boots

Good *leather* backcountry boots are sturdy, torsionally rigid hiking boots with an extended sole for clipping into the binding toepiece. The leather is rigid enough to provide support yet flexible enough for comfort. Unlike a pair of downhill ski boots, you can walk comfortably in your backcountry ski boots. The soles of the boots are stiff torsionally—if you can flex the boot by twisting it torsionally at the toe and heel, it is much too soft. You need a stiff boot to transfer

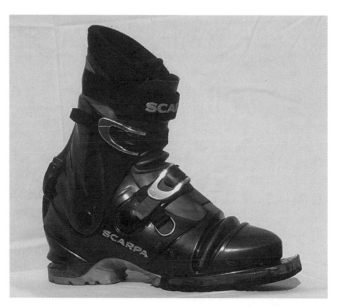

Good boots are critical to your ski performance.
Plastic boots, like these T-2s from Scarpa, keep your
feet dry.

the turning power of your legs directly to the ski. The torsional rigidity gives you the control you need to steer your skis through a turn.

Leather backcountry boots come in single and double thickness. The double boots have an inner layer of insulation that adds warmth but also adds weight. If you suffer from chronically cold feet, consider buying a pair of double boots. A more versatile solution to the problem of cold feet is to buy a pair of single boots and combine them with a rubber randed insulated supergaiter that covers the entire boot.

Plastic Telemark Boots

In 1992 the Scarpa Boot Company unveiled the first all-plastic backcountry ski boots, and the off-piste skiing world was forever changed. Jokingly called the "Terminator" because it set out to make leather boots history, Scarpa's all-plastic buckle boot lived up to its name and delivered the goods by providing more power and control to telemark skiers of all abilities. Indeed, so revolutionary was the

Terminator, one backcountry ski magazine called it "the invention of the decade."

The Terminator and its copycats from Garmont and other companies are relatively lightweight, completely waterproof, and extremely comfortable even on long tours. Too, they allow for a more aggressive and exciting style, further blurring whatever distinctions remain between alpine and nordic skiing. No longer limited by flimsy gear but rather armed with plastic boots, wide skis, and beefy free-heal cable bindings, free-heel skiers are ripping lines down the steepest faces in the farthest ranges.

Whether you choose leather or plastic, make sure your boots are neither too large nor too small. Large boots will give you blisters; tight boots are iceboxes because they constrict the flow of blood to your feet. If you can get two pairs of wool socks inside them and your feet feel comfortably snug but not tight, you have a good fit.

Other Boots

Unless you do all your winter camping in the mountains, there will be times when you won't need a stiff boot for backcountry skiing. Say you are planning to ski the frozen waterways of Minnesota's Boundary Waters, or ski to the North or South Pole for that matter. On flat surfaces in extremely cold conditions, the best choice is a pair of mukluks. These soft, Native American boots are ideal for winter camping and skiing where a rigid boot is not critical.

Plastic mountaineering boots are the footwear of choice for trips into alpine areas.

Mukluks are lightweight, one-piece moccasins that reach to just under the knee. Just insert a wool duffel sock or a felt liner, put on a couple of pairs of warm socks, and lace them up. Mukluks are lighter than leather boots and also much warmer. Flexible and breathable, mukluks are a real treat for your feet—it's like skiing in a pair of toasty warm slippers. Steger Mukluks in Minnesota makes a model with breathable uppers and rubberized elk hide soles that work beautifully with both skis and snowshoes.

BINDINGS

Many backcountry skiers who use leather boots and lightweight touring or backcountry skis find that the traditional 75MM "Nordic Norm" three-pin binding that has been around forever is perfectly suited to their needs. The Backcountry "seventy-fives" are much stronger than the typical 75MM touring binding. They are strong enough to withstand the pressure of cutting moderate turns, and beefy enough to support a heavy-duty, leather backcountry boot. Also, the wide, flat bails that clamp down the toe of the boot on the backcountry 75MM bindings are much stronger than the wire bails of touring bindings, which can break under the stresses of a backcountry touring ski trip. Unless you want to spend all your time fixing your gear, don't try to use touring bindings on your winter camping trips.

Those backcountry skiers and winter campers who merely wish to glide on the flats and tour in the mountains may want to try the "backcountry" or "BC" bindings offered by Salomon and Rotte-fella. These bindings attach directly to a wide metal bar inserted across the bottom of the boot toe. Perfectly adequate for general touring, the "BC" bindings simply do not offer the control or the power of either a standard three-pin or, especially, a cable binding.

Along with wide skis and plastic boots, cable bindings have revolutionized the backcountry skiing scene. Indeed, with the advent of beefier boots made to power ever wider skis, the standard three-pin binding just can't handle the greater forces generated by the more powerful equipment. Aggressive skiers who used plastic boots with three-pin bindings no sooner made a few hard turns than they began ripping the old seventy-fives right out of their skis. The equipment manufacturers responded by producing heftier binding with strong heel cables.

Mukluks are ideal for snowshoeing.

The cable binding, a revised version of the old binding many of us used as kids, puts less stress on your boot because it is not held by pins at the toe alone but by a cable that goes around the back of the heel and keeps the front of the boot secure in the toepiece. The cables offer increased lateral stability because the entire boot is held securely in the grip of the cable, eliminating any trace of side-to-side motion, and they are more easily fixed or improvised if they break than three-pin bindings.

POLES

If you are old enough, you probably remember those horrible bamboo twigs with the cheap grips and leather straps that used to be the only choice of backcountry ski poles. When those things broke, they didn't just fracture, they splintered into a fan of bamboo shards—and they broke all the time.

Fortunately things have changed, and the bamboo sticks are not the only ones available. Today, poles are receiving the same meticulous attention that has revolutionized cross-country ski gear across the board. Poles are now available in high-tech synthetic fibers and metal alloys that are incredibly strong and lightweight. Today there are some fine poles out there for the backcountry skier.

When choosing a pole, look for strength, weight, and fit. The stiffer your pole, the more power you put into your skiing as you thrust the pole into the snow and push off. A stiff pole propels you forward, whereas a soft pole absorbs your energy and bends. A lightweight pole requires less energy to swing back and forth all day long—an important consideration on a multiday tour.

Proper fit depends on what kind of skiing you do. Most skiers prefer a pole that comes up to the armpit. Some skiers prefer a pole that reaches the top of the shoulder. I find both these measurements too long for backcountry skiing. Long poles can be very awkward on downhill runs.

A good solution to the length problem is an adjustable pole specifically designed for backcountry skiers-a pole that you can extend while skiing on the flats, shorten for the downhill run, and join together to create an avalanche probe. For the serious backcountry skier, these adjustable poles are a worthwhile investment, especially if you plan on traveling in the mountains or in avalanche country.

While many skiers and winter campers choose to use their regular touring poles, the important point to remember is pole strength. You don't want your pole to bend or collapse when you trust it with all your weight, and you don't want it to shatter ten miles into your trip and ruin your day. It pays to get a good set of poles.

Pole baskets have evolved too, and now you can get a variety of configurations—ovals, half circles, stars—but the best all-around basket for the backcountry is still the old circle because it provides the most flotation in deep, unbroken snow.

OTHER SKI GEAR

Climbing skins. In the old days, climbing skins were just that: ski-length strips of animal hide that skiers attached to the bottom of their skis. With the hairs pointing toward the tail of the ski, the skins gave the skis a tenacious grip on steep uphills when the skier pressed down on the ski. At the top the skier simply ripped the hides from the bottoms of his skis and continued on his way.

Today, climbing skins are made of synthetic fibers, but they perform the same function as the original hides. As the ski glides forward, the hairs provide little resistance. If the ski starts to slip backwards, the hairs dig into the snow and hold.

Without skins, many routes commonly enjoyed by backcountry skiers would be inaccessible. The skins are essential to get up any trail that is more than moderately steep. Also, as you climb you can run into transition snow. Skins keep you from climbing out of the range of your wax and bogging down.

Knee pads. When you're five days from medical help, the best medicine is prevention, and the easiest way to avoid smashing a kneecap on a buried rock or stump is to wear a pair of telemark knee pads. When you ski the backcountry your knees cannot avoid coming into contact with the snow, your skis, or other objects. These little insurance policies are sold in specialty ski shops and are designed so you can put them on over or under your ski pants without removing your ski boots.

Ski leashes. Leashes attach your binding to your boot. Not all skiers use them in the backcountry, but they keep your skis from running away in the event of a binding release. Also, when you go to a ski area to sharpen your skills, you'll be required to use them.

SNOWSHOES

The snowshoe, like the wheel, is one of those creations that revolutionized human life. Before the first snowshoes were invented thousands of years ago, people simply couldn't live in parts of the globe that were substantially snow covered. They would have floundered in the white stuff, unable to travel, to hunt, to move with the seasons or the game. The "raquettes," as the French Canadian fur traders called them, enabled people to move around in areas previously inaccessible.

Nothing has changed in the intervening years. If you want to travel in snow country, you need a way to stay afloat over the drifts. Skis are one way, snowshoes are another.

Credit the northern forest Native Americans with perfecting the snowshoe. Unlike the Eskimos, who for the most part live in a landscape of hard, wind-packed snow and ice where snowshoes aren't really necessary, Native Americans inhabit more temperate latitudes, areas where the winters are long and the snows pile high. For them, snowshoes are an essential means of transportation.

Snowshoes come in all sorts of shapes and sizes, but the variety of forms is not just the result of different artistic sensibilities. They are different because they are designed to perform specific functions. As with skis, the design characteristics determine the strengths and weaknesses of the various models. But before we discuss particular designs, let's look at general characteristics.

Snowshoe materials haven't changed much over the years the way ski materials have. The two widely available choices are wood and metal, each having its own advantages and disadvantages. For most uses, traditional white ash wood is still the material of choice. There are several reasons for this, including tradition, aesthetics, and feel—wood has a springiness to it, a liveliness, that metal shoes have yet to duplicate. Wood is strong and supple, flexing under stress yet providing the stability and support you need. Both wood and metal snowshoes are available in a wide variety of shapes, sizes, and modifications.

For trips in the mountains, metal snowshoes can't be beat. The metal frames give them incredible strength and durability. Virtually impossible to break in the field, metal snowshoes are safe and very reliable in the roughest terrain. Even when bridged between rocks

Metal showshoes are reliable in rough terrain.

while supporting the full weight of the climber and his or her gear, they will not bend or break.

Also, metal mountaineering shoes have a traction aid situated beneath the ball of the foot that acts just like a crampon. Two types of traction aid are commonly available, and both provide plenty of grip. The first is a serrated metal triangle for moderate climbs, the other is a more lethal looking crampon with six 1 1/2-inch triangular teeth—a lot of bite for more extreme conditions.

Snowshoe webbing (also called lacing, filling, or decking) is the netting that is attached to the snowshoe frames to support the weight of the snowshoer over the snow. The webbing must be made of a tough, tight, abrasion-resistant material. The pattern of the webbing depends upon snow conditions. The weaving of the pattern will be very close for a shoe used in light, fine frost/snow and more open for a shoe used in coarse or wind-packed snow.

There are two basic types of webbing, including babiche, or rawhide, and neoprene. Babiche is the traditional choice. Native Americans use the hides of beaver, bear, caribou, and moose. Commercial babiche is usually steer hide. While remaining popular, it is not foolproof. Babiche soaks up water when used in heavy, wet snow, and the laces sag under these conditions. To prevent this from becoming a problem they must be treated annually with a waterproofing varnish.

Neoprene, a rubber-coated nylon, is generally acknowledged as the superior filling because, unlike babiche, neoprene does not soak up moisture, nor does it stretch or sag when wet or from use. Neoprene is very strong, resists decay, and appears to last longer than babiche. Still, it is not perfect. Coarse snow or crust can fray the neoprene, causing snow to collect and freeze to the frayed strands. These must be clipped or burned off, otherwise you will end up carrying around a lot of extra weight.

Choose your snowshoes according to your needs: a shoe that will match the terrain, snow conditions, and your weight. Is your trip primarily a steep mountain route or will you wade through the deep snows of the interior forests? Will you be in heavy brush or on the snowy, wind-packed surfaces of lakes and rivers? Ask yourself these questions. There is a snowshoe design best suited to every type of terrain.

Snowshoe designs range from the flat, circular shoes with a very fine weave used by the Naskapi, Cree, and Montagnais Indians

An underfoot tractor aid can be a big help in climbing with snowshoes.

of Quebec and Labrador to the long, narrow snowshoes used by Kutchin and Koyukon Indians of interior Alaska. Key characteristics of snowshoes include:

Width. The more surface area a snowshoe has, the more flotation over the snow it provides. This is especially true when combined with a fine-weave webbing. A wide snowshoe can also be short, making it more maneuverable in brush.

Length. When crossing open country where maneuverability is not a problem, a long snowshoe provides equal surface area to a wide shoe, and thus approximately equal flotation, but is easier to go quickly with because it is narrow and long, like a ski.

Weave. The finer the weave, the more the shoe will float atop the snow surface.

Tip. An upturned tip will let the snowshoe tip rise clear of the depression it makes in the snow without catching. This is an especially helpful feature on steep uphills.

Tail. The tails of longer snowshoes help keep the snowshoes tracking in a straight line. Also, they provide a counterweight to the tips, so that when you lift the snowshoe, the tails drag on the snow behind and the tips rise above the snow.

TYPES OF SNOWSHOES

The wide, circular snowshoe used by the Naskapi, Cree, and Montagnais Indians of eastern Canada is excellent for use in areas of deep snow and heavy brush—the fine weave and extreme width keep it from sinking, while the short length makes maneuvering easy. It has a flat tip and may have a slight tail.

The Alaska shoe, a long, narrow snowshoe, is at home in the deep powder of more open country. With an overall surface area equivalent to the Naskapi shoe, the Alaska shoe floats well, but the relative narrowness of its width combined with its extreme length make this model perform more like a ski in open country. The long tail of the Alaska shoe helps it track in a straight line. The upturned toe keeps the tips from diving into the snow with every step.

In between these extreme designs are the snowshoes commonly available in sporting goods and outdoors stores. The most popular and most versatile models incorporate characteristics of both the Naskapi and Alaskan models. As with backcountry skis, the most effective models for general use are hybrids.

The standard bearpaw is a short, wide, tailless shoe without an upturned toe—features that make it simple and extremely maneuverable. Its balance and short length preclude the need for an upturned tip and a tail. The bearpaw is small, lightweight, and is at home in deep snow, thick brush, and hilly terrain. Because of its versatility, the bearpaw is popular with trappers and others who work in the woods.

The modified, or Green Mountain bearpaw, is a slightly longer and slightly narrower version of the standard bearpaw. Like the standard bearpaw, the Green Mountain is at home in a variety of conditions and is perhaps the most popular model for general use.

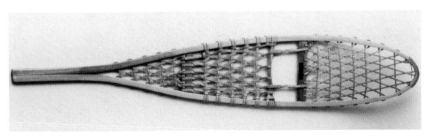

Classic designs for wooden snowshoes: the Alaska snowshoe

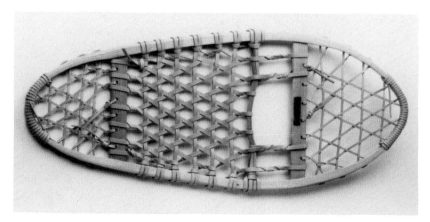

the standard Bearpaw...

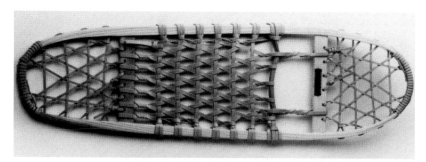

the Green Mountain Bearpaw...

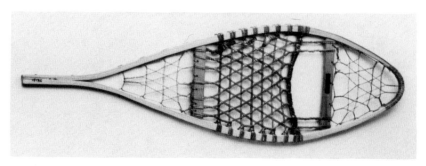

and the Maine or Michigan snowshoe.
Photos courtesy Tubbs Snowshoes

The Maine, or Michigan, snowshoe is the model most people envision when they think of snowshoes. Teardrop shaped, the Maine starts out wide in front, tapers back to a tail in the rear, and has an upturned toe. The Maine is a cross between the Alaska and the bearpaw and incorporates many good qualities of both. The Maine snowshoe is an excellent choice for carrying heavy loads in a wide variety of conditions.

WHAT SIZE SNOWSHOE?

The size snowshoe you'll need will depend on where you plan to travel and what types of snow conditions you expect. The area covered by your snowshoe and the closeness of the webbing weave are what provide you with flotation in deep snow. The wider the area and the closer the weave, the greater the amount of flotation. So if you plan to travel in an area where cold, light snow conditions prevail, you will need a wider, more closely woven snowshoe than you would for a trip in hard-packed conditions.

Snowshoe manufacturers provide charts matching snowshoe sizes to your weight to help you choose frame size. Use these charts only as a guideline. When you select a snowshoe, don't forget to add the weight you will be carrying on your back to your body weight. You may carry fifty pounds or more on a winter camping trip, so make sure to get a snowshoe that is beefy enough for the job.

SNOWSHOE BINDINGS

Like a cross-country ski binding, the snowshoe binding keeps the foot secured to the snowshoe while allowing the heel to lift with every step.

Traditional bindings are made of a length of lamp wicking tied in a pattern around the heel and toe called the "squaw hitch." The squaw hitch is still the lightest, simplest binding, but tying it has become something of a lost skill among the majority of winter campers. In recent years bindings that lack the simplicity but provide more support have gained in popularity among recreational snowshoers.

Modern snowshoe bindings consist of a toepiece, a heel strap, and an instep strap. There are basically two types of snowshoe bindings: rigid and flexible. Rigid bindings offer greater control and are an excellent choice for mountain travelers. But for those people whose feet angle radically in or out, the rigid binding can cause the snowshoes to touch or overlap when walking with a normal stride. For those people with toes that point in or out, a flexible binding is probably a better choice. Flexible binding don't force the foot to remain in a straight line atop the snowshoe. Instead, they allow the user to walk naturally while the snowshoes swing clear of and parallel to each other at every step.

SNOWSHOE FOOTWEAR

Unlike ski boots, snowshoeing footwear is not specialized. Snowshoe racers, preferring a light, quick step, sometimes use running shoes. On expedition, however, the two major considerations are weight and warmth, and if you want the warmest, lightest boot around, choose mukluks. Find a pair with a rubberized sole for added traction for when you aren't wearing the snowshoes. Most types of hide or pack cloth can be quite slippery on the snow.

Skiers and mountaineers who carry snowshoes for occasional bouts with deep snow will be fine using their ski or mountaineering boots. Many winter campers use pacs, felt-lined boots with leather uppers and rubber bottoms. These boots are warm and comfortable, but they are also very heavy. A rule of thumb is that a pound on your feet is equivalent to five on your back, so if you choose pacs over mukluks, plan on carrying around a lot of extra weight for no gain in warmth.

summary checklist: gear for travel

Skis
* Waxless
* Waxable
* Metal edges
* Single camber
* Double camber

Ski Bindings
* Three–pin 75MM backcountry
* Cable binding
* Binding for mukluks (such as Berwin)

Snowshoes
* Alaska
* Bearpaw
* Green Mountain (modified Bearpaw)
* Maine (or Michigan)
* Naskapi

Snowshoe Bindings
* Super A binding
* H binding
* Squaw hitch

Ski Footwear
* Telemark ski boots
* Mukluks

Snowshoe Footwear
* Mukluks
* Felt–lined pacs

Mountaineering Footwear
* Rigid double moun– taineering boots (leather or plastic)

Poles
* Telescoping to join into avalanche probes
* Round baskets

Climbing Skins
* Synthetic mohair or plastic

Knee Pads

Ski Leash

Crampons (see p. 129)
* 10– or 12–point hinged
* Ridged (for rigid mountaineering boots only)

Ice Axe (see pp. 129– 132)

7.
Food and Nutrition

GUIDES HAVE THEIR FOLK HEROES TOO, you know—the more colorful the better. And Alferd Packer is many a mountain guide's hero—a man as colorful as his name is twisted. His exploits earned him everlasting fame. He even became a patron saint of the Colorado Republican party.

The story goes that in 1873 Alferd was hired to guide a hunting party in the Colorado Rockies. During a blizzard, Alferd and five of his guests became lost and snowbound. When spring arrived, down from the mountains came Alferd, fit and well fed, none the worse for his ordeal. But his five clients were nowhere to be found. Search parties soon discovered the macabre remains of the five missing hunters, each showing definite signs of foul play.

Packer was arrested, of course, and charged with cannibalism. So far, admittedly, there is nothing truly unusual about this story—what's a hungry guide to do? But what the judge declared when he found Packer guilty launched the demented mountaineer into immortality:

"Alferd Packer," said the judge, "you voracious man-eating son of a bitch. There were only seven Democrats in Hinsdale County, and you ate five of them!"

Fear not. The chances are excellent that your meals won't be quite so exotic. They will, however, be nutritious, filling, and—if you use your imagination—never boring! If you think winter camping food consists of cold oatmeal, gruel, and mush, you are in for a surprise. Read on.

You can't overstate how important food is on a winter camping trip. Food supplies you with the energy you need to travel all day and stay warm all night. When you get enough of the right foods to eat, you'll be healthy, happy, and ready to go. Good meals go a long way toward ensuring high morale and top physical performance.

You need a lot of food in the winter woods. That faceless character, the average American, consumes some 2,700 calories per day while living a largely sedentary life. This is too much when just sitting around, and he or she tends to get a little chubby (some might say a lot chubby). But 2,700 calories is a starvation diet for anyone on the winter trail. Too little food and you risk fatigue and hypothermia.

How many calories do you need to carry a pack or pull a sled in the cold for eight or nine hours a day? You can start figuring around 4,000 calories per person per day and bump it up from there. That translates into about two to two-and-a-half pounds of food per person per day (less if you use freeze-dried foods). Don't worry about eating too much, I've never known anyone to gain weight on a winter camping trip. In fact, it can be a great way to trim off any excess.

As a general rule, you don't need to pack fresh fruits and vegetables. That's good news, because it is impossible for reasons of preservation and weight to bring more than minimal supplies of fresh food along. What is important, however, is to represent three major food groups in your daily menu planning.

As a rule of thumb, 50 percent of your food intake should be in the form of carbohydrates, which give your body quick, efficient energy. Foods such as sugar or honey, rice, pasta, and cereal are excellent sources of carbohydrates.

About 20 percent of your food should be proteins, from meats, cheese, milk, grains, beans, and nuts. Proteins are important for cell maintenance and growth.

The remaining 30 percent or so (remember, individual needs vary) should be in the form of fat. Fats contain more than twice the calories per pound than either proteins or carbohydrates, making them essential, efficient foods for packing into the winter wilderness. Foods that contain fat are butter and margarine, cooking oil, salami, pepperoni, sausage, cheese, nuts, and peanut butter. One experi-

Plenty of good food is vital on a winter camping excursion. (Elk Range, CO)

enced winter traveler satisfies his body's craving for fats by munching on sticks of butter as if they were candy bars!

Vitamins and minerals will be well represented if you plan a well-balanced diet from the foods listed above. Water-soluble vitamins—the B and C groups—can be replenished daily by bringing vitamin-fortified fruit drinks or by bringing along a supply of vitamins from home.

A last word on variety. You can eat the same healthy and filling meal every day and meet your nutritional requirements, but your stomach will rebel if you don't provide it with a change now and then. Try to build in different textures, flavors, and smells when you put your meal plan together.

WHAT FOOD TO BRING

How meticulous do you need to be in planning for the three major food groups? Not very. Basically, you can eat what you eat at home, just more of it. Do you plan your daily meals at home with a USDA chart? I suspect not. If you are an active person, you know what your body needs. What you must take into consideration beyond nutritional concerns, however, is the weight and the bulk of your food supplies.

Meal suggestions are provided, but I suggest you take a look at the following list of basic ingredients and use your imagination in combining them into your own tasty concoctions. You can either plan meals ahead of time or bring along the raw materials and get creative in the field.

Fresh foods. Avoid fresh foods for the most part. Because of their high water content they tend to be heavy and spoil quickly. Exceptions are butter and cheese; baked goods such as cookies and brownies (which can be made in advance or on the trail); nuts; and meats such as salami and pepperoni. These foods take up less space than, say, fresh eggs, fruits, and vegetables; and they provide plenty of concentrated nutrition for their weight.

Dry foods. The bulk of your food will be dry—foods with 95 percent or more of the water removed. When it's time to eat, you reconstitute them with water you've brought or melted snow. These nonperishables lighten the load and are available at any neighborhood grocery store. They include mixed dried vegetables; also dried onion, garlic, and potatoes; sunflower seeds and soybeans; egg or whole-grain pastas such as spaghetti, macaroni, and noodles; and Ramen noodle packets.

Also bring grains—rice, cracked wheat, corn, and oatmeal (granola and other cereals make wonderful hot breakfasts; throw in some nuts, raisins, and a spoonful of butter or margarine along with some honey or brown sugar)—beans and lentils; spices and herbs;

dried milk; fruits such as raisins, peaches, and apricots; and lots of soup and sauce mixes for bases and added flavoring.

Available in your local grocery store are prepackaged dried dinners that are lightweight and easy to prepare. These meals can be quite fancy, with such repasts as beef Stroganoff and fettuccine Alfredo on the menu. They are more expensive, but the savings in weight and time may make them worth it to you. As with all prepackaged foods, don't believe the number of suggested servings on the box. If it says "serves eight," it might just make a meal for two hungry winter campers.

Freeze-dried foods. Freeze-dried foods are extremely lightweight and require only minimal preparation and cooking time. Most you merely soak in hot water for a few minutes and—voila! Shrimp creole! As a longtime skeptic of these mealtime miracles, I was completely won over by freeze-dried food while on a winter traverse of New Hampshire's Presidential Range.

During the four-day crossing we endured gales and subzero temperatures. In those extreme conditions the last thing anyone wanted to do was play Julia Child. Not only did the freeze-dried dinners weigh almost nothing—enabling us to move rapidly over the

Pack a variety of lightweight dry foods along with snacks and plenty of hot drink mixes.

exposed mountain summits—they were truly delicious and provided excellent nutrition.

Extras. Don't forget the little extras to spice things up and add some zip to your creations! Add soup, sauce mixes, and bouillon cubes to meals for enhanced flavor. Honey, syrup, and brown sugar provide lots of calories and taste. And bring along some popcorn for a fun after-dinner snack.

Herbs and spices. Jazz up your meals with a small selection of herbs and spices, too. Salt and pepper; cayenne; garlic and onion; cumin; chili powder; and Italian seasoning weigh only an ounce or so and can make the difference between a so-so meal and a culinary delight. Pack them in 35MM film canisters and label them. Clear plastic film canisters are best because you can see what's in them before you dump it on your food.

One-pot simplicity. Simplicity is a blessing on a winter camping trip, so using one large pot for cooking makes the most sense. That way all of the ingredients are already combined, making preparation easy, with only minimal cleaning, leaving you free to travel farther, explore around camp, or relax around the campfire and enjoy a hot drink.

And keep the hot drinks coming! Another pot can be used as a hot water supply for cocoa, coffee, and regular or herbal tea. Add a lump of butter or margarine to your hot drink for some extra energy to keep you warm. I can't conceive of not starting and ending my day with lots of hot drinks.

WHAT ABOUT LUNCH?

There are two ways to have lunch, maybe more. One way is to begin lunch right after breakfast and keep eating until dinner. You need lots of energy on the trail, so eat plenty and often.

For munching on the trail some people pack gorp (good old raisins and peanuts—with M&M's®, of course) in a resealable bag. Others bring along some cut-up cheese and salami or sausage sticks (cutting cheese or sausage in advance before they freeze is a good idea). When everyone packs a different item, you can mix and match. If you choose this mobile method of eating lunch, make sure the foods you bring along are easily packed and are accessible.

The other way to have lunch is more relaxed. Find a place out of the wind, in the sun, overlooking some scenic vista, and stop. If it's cold, bundle up, start a stove, and make hot drinks. If you really want to do it right, build a small fire and relax on your sleeping pad. Take off your boots and socks and warm your toes. Dig into your pack and have a handful of gorp. Sharpen a stick and roast some sausage or pepperoni to bring out the flavor. Put a pot of water on and boil up a pail of tea. What's the rush? This is living!

PACKING EFFICIENTLY

It happens every trip. Eight o'clock, cold and dark, everybody's hungry, and the cook is frantically trying to locate the macaroni and cheese. Soon everyone is rooting through stuff sacks, headlamp beams search out the lost meal supplies, tempers flash in the night.

"I thought you had all the dinners!"

"And I thought you had set aside everything we needed for today's meals!"

"Why don't you two shut up! We need to devise a better system so we don't go through this every night!"

Once you have purchased the food, remove all the packaging. You can save an incredible amount of weight and bulk by stripping off all the cardboard and plastic. Better yet, purchase your food in bulk at a co-op. Repack the food in plastic bags—the kind you get at your local supermarket produce section work well and can double as vapor-barrier socks. Use double bags to make sure the food doesn't spill out. Save any cooking instructions from the boxes and put them in the bags with the food. Identify what is in the bag with a bold marking pen. Remember, cornmeal, pancake mix, dried milk, and lemonade powder all look alike in the dark.

If the bags are long enough, twist the tops and tie a slip knot to seal them. Overhand knots are impossible to undo. Metal twist-ties already carpet the ground around many campsites. Keep them out of the woods.

You can save a lot of time if you mix your meals in advance and package them before you begin your trip. You can even plan on when you will eat them and mark the bag accordingly. A bag marked "D-2" for instance, means "dinner, day 2."

Now what do you do with that mound of food? One way to get a handle on it is to pack each meal in separate stuff sacks, so all the breakfasts are together, for instance, likewise with the lunches and dinners. Pack condiments and extras in their own stuff sack. With this method, you only need to find one stuff sack at mealtime. If you color-code the stuff sacks—say yellow is for breakfast, red for dinner—you'll be that much more efficient. Use as many stuff sacks as there are people to distribute the weight evenly.

Another less scientific way is to divide the pile of food into equal portions according to the number of people. Then, plan the next day's meals ahead of time and put everything you will need for that day—breakfast, lunch, dinner—in a separate stuff sack. This method requires daily reorganization but works, too.

FOOD CACHES

Setting up food caches can be a great way to lighten your load and extend your range. If you are going out for ten days to a couple of weeks or more, you need to think seriously about resupplying along the way.

Take a look at your proposed route. Are there places where you cross a road or intersect a hiking trail? Find accessible spots that are five to ten days apart, and set up your caches. Drive and then hike in to the spot and set up your cache.

Make sure that your supplies are well packed—impermeable to moisture, in rugged containers—and are well hidden. The last thing you need is to arrive at a cache and find that it has been tampered with.

Double-bag your supplies in plastic, then place them inside sealed plastic containers—the kind doughnut shops use to ship filling work well. They are the size of a large bucket and are made of heavy-duty plastic with gasket-sealed tops. Many shops will sell them to you for a dollar or so. You can place these buckets inside heavy-duty plastic garbage bags for further protection.

Camouflage your caches well. You can hang or cover them. Whatever you do, make sure *you* know where they are. Locate each cache on your maps like a buried treasure—X marks the spot! Include a note in the cache addressed to anyone who might discover it, telling them what it is for and asking them not to tamper with it.

Besides food, you can stock your cache with dry socks, matches, batteries, and maps for the next section of your trip. You can even include a flask of something special. Be creative! Just be sure to return to all of your cache sites after the trip and clean up everything you left behind.

Another way to cache your food is to chip a trench in the ice of a frozen lake or river. Place your items in the trench, then fill the trench with water. The water will freeze in a matter of minutes, and your supplies will be safely sealed in the ice until you chip them out.

WATER

Cold winter air is extremely dry, and because of this your moisture loss is more acute in winter than in summer. Replenish the water you lose through perspiration and breathing by drinking constantly.

While you may not feel thirsty, force yourself to drink before you become dehydrated. Drink three or four quarts of water every day, and you'll feel more energetic and healthier during your trip. Dehydration leads to depression, lethargy, chills, and hypothermia. An easy way to tell if you are getting enough water is to check your urine. If it is dark, you need to drink more.

suggested foods for winter camping

Breakfast
* Hot cocoa/Coffee/Tea
* Powdered fruit drinks
* Cereals/Granola
* Oatmeal/Hot Cereals
* Powdered milk
* Dried fruits
* Pancakes
* Muffins
* Bannock bread
* Sausage, bacon, or ham
* Butter or margarine
* Brown sugar
* Honey
* Maple syrup

Lunch
* Pepperoni or sausage
* Cheese
* Gorp
* Crackers
* Cookies
* Chocolate/Candy bars
* Dried fruits
* Bagels
* Peanut butter
* Soups
* Hot cocoa/Coffee/Tea

Dinner
* Macaroni and cheese
* Spaghetti
* Noodle casseroles
* Freeze–dried dinners

Dinner (cont.)
* Prepackaged dinners
* Rice
* Cracked wheat
* Beans/Lentils
* Potato flakes
* Vegetable flakes
* Tuna
* Cheese
* Sausage, bacon, or ham
* Soup mixes
* Instant sauces
* Bouillon cubes
* Butter or margarine
* Cooking oil

Desserts
* Cakes
* Brownies
* Cookies
* Pies
* Cheesecake
* Pudding

Extras
* Nuts/Sunflower seeds
* Soy beans
* Wheat germ
* Raisins/Dried fruits
* Popcorn
* Instant sauces
* Bouillon cubes
* Spices
* Soy sauce

8.
On Trail

·········

"**THIS IS IT,**" you say quietly to yourself, stealing a quick glance around to see how the others are doing, to see if they feel the same nervous excitement that you do. Hard to tell—everyone is so intent on arranging their packs, lacing boots, and putting on gaiters.

You get out of the car and feel the fresh breeze cool against your cheek, follow the snow-covered trail with your eyes into the forest to where it disappears. You linger for a moment, reluctant to give up the warmth and safety of the vehicle. With a flash you see that you are astride a margin, about to cross a boundary into the unknown. Suddenly, you understand that this trip is no longer theoretical. One more step and you are committed. "Everybody ready? Okay, let's go!"

After about ten seconds, apprehension turns to exhilaration. The simple act of moving engenders powerful feelings of freedom, joy, and wonder. You have crossed the barrier, all doubts are gone, replaced by sheer excitement.

For the first half hour or so you burn up the track, carried by adrenaline and excitement. But after awhile you adjust to the new surroundings. The car and the road are far behind. Life settles down to a more natural rhythm. You feel the first flush of heat, know that you are about to break a sweat, and stop. Time to take off a layer or two, slow down, and move along at a regular pace.

Find a comfortable pace that you can keep up all day without needing to stop. Going full tilt until your legs feel like lead, your

·····

lungs are on fire, and your heart is thumping like a battering ram is no way to enjoy yourself. When you stop, it should be to take a drink of water, shed or add a layer, look at the map, or grab a handful of gorp. Stopping to rest is a sure sign that you are moving too quickly.

It's important to realize that for the first day or two you'll be adjusting to a whole new world and way of living. Give yourself a chance to get acclimated, not only to your surroundings but to your equipment as well. Don't try to cover too much ground the first day or so, but leave time for adjusting your clothing and packing systems, fiddling with bindings and waxes, and setting up camp in the light.

In those first days, thermo-regulation is critical. We're talking about layering again. Remember, the trick is to stay dry. Most beginner winter campers cannot fathom only needing a layer or two while on the trail, but it's true. Much of the time you are moving along, you'll wear only your long underwear tops and bottoms, and perhaps shell pants.

While in camp, before heading out in the morning, anticipate how much clothing you'll need after ten minutes of vigorous hiking or skiing, and strip down before you set out. After a few minutes the chill will be replaced by a luxurious warm glow as your muscles warm up to the task ahead. And if you need to stop and take off another layer, do it, don't be shy. Better to make a few adjustments early on than to get soaked.

Keep all your layers dry! Brush snow off of everything. If it is snowing, put on your shell. If you stop for lunch in the sun or build a small fire, take advantage of the heat to dry your clothes. Never let a drying opportunity pass by.

Staying together is another vital practice. There are times you'll want to spread out, give each other some space, and ski or snowshoe alone for awhile. On these occasions you can really tune in to your environment. Look around and listen, learn what the wilderness has to teach. But always stay within sight and sound of each other.

An easy way to stay in touch is if everyone takes responsibility for the person directly behind. This way, from front to back there is an unbroken line of communication. If anyone needs to stop to shed a layer or take a drink, the whole group should pause. No one gets left behind.

Adjust your layers to keep from becoming too cold—or too hot.
(Elk Range, CO)

When traveling in potentially hazardous places the group should keep close together in case help is needed. There will be times, as when you cross thin ice or a possible avalanche chute, when communication will be vital. At these and other times the group needs to work together as a team.

The group must travel at the pace of the slowest member. If the group exceeds this pace, the slow member will become fatigued and more susceptible to illness or injury.

How do you keep the slowest person from becoming demoralized or from dropping too far behind? Let that person lead the group for a while. The psychological boost a person gets from being out in front, breaking trail in fresh snow, can have an enormously beneficial effect. Especially when approaching a summit or open vista, let the person who spends most of the time in the rear have a chance to get there first. The view from up front can be a lot more interesting than the scene from the rear.

Rotating the person in the lead can accomplish another purpose as well: breaking trail. If the snow is deep, this can be an exhausting chore. One way to spread out the work is to travel single file. When the person in front gets tired, she steps to the side and lets the rest of the group pass, taking her new position at the rear. By the time the rest of the group members have done their turn at the front of the line, she should be well enough rested from skiing or snowshoeing on a broken trail to take over the lead position again.

Another way to break trail is to lighten the load of one group member by dividing his heavy food and equipment among the rest of the group, then let him go ahead and break the trail for his more heavily burdened teammates. The light pack can be traded around so everyone has a chance to give to the effort. When everyone takes a turn breaking trail, all members feel they are contributing to the overall goals of the group.

The best way for the group to avoid trouble and have a pleasant trip is for everyone to be aware. Preventing injuries is vital on any trip but is especially so in winter. Through acute awareness of your surroundings and of each other, you can greatly enhance your chances for an incident-free experience.

Take turns breaking trail in deep snow.
(Maine Woods)

When you are aware, you can read the signals nature is sending. For example: dark or discolored snow on the surface of a river or lake speaks of thin ice or overflowing water. A ring around the moon tells of an approaching snowstorm. A steep, open snow gully through a forested slope is delivering a lecture on avalanches. Snow streamers blowing off a summit carry the message of windchill and certain frostbite for uncovered skin.

There are many indications of potential trouble, many clues to the right path. Listen to your surroundings, and listen to each other, too. A person cannot see the whiteness on their cheeks or nose, which means frostbite. Someone else must be aware. And if someone complains of being tired, cold, or hungry, that is a clear indication something is amiss and must be dealt with immediately, before complications develop. Look around, keep your eyes and ears open, and be aware. Someone is trying to tell you something.

NAVIGATION WITH MAP AND COMPASS

Moving confidently through the wilderness toward a destination, knowing exactly where you are the entire time, is called navigation. No one is born with the ability to navigate a course through unknown territory. That requires skill and training.

With a map, compass, and awareness of his surroundings, a wilderness traveler is never lost, even though he may be seeing the country for the first time. Striking off in any direction and letting go of the security of roads, crowds, even trails, is a liberating feeling. All it takes to feel at home in the wild is the right tools and a sense of where you are.

In the United States, finding true wilderness to navigate is becoming more difficult every year. Outside of Alaska, there are perhaps a handful of places more than a dozen miles from a road, and that number is shrinking. Our national forests are crisscrossed by a labyrinth of logging roads, our national parks are home to a network of scenic drives and visitors' concessions. Even our official wilderness areas are liberally laced with maintained footpaths and sprinkled with trail signs. The ability to navigate in unmarked terrain can get you off trail and into those last reserves of truly wild country. Indeed, navigation may soon be the art of "getting lost"—getting away from it all!

The first step toward becoming a skilled navigator is to develop your powers of observation. Notice which way the streams run, where the lakes are, and if any hills or mountains rise above the surrounding landscape. Notice gaps, or passes, between the ranges. Keep an eye out for areas devoid of vegetation, such as bogs, meadows, or open summits. Turn completely around and observe how these landmarks appear when you approach them from another direction. Watch the sun rise in the east and set in the west. The moon does the same. So do the stars. And the North Star hangs over the Pole, making it an exceptional navigational aid.

Consult your map during rest breaks to pinpoint your location. (Wind River Range, WY)

The landscape is a complex maze, but there is a pattern and a rhythm to it. Immerse yourself in it, and observe. Try to understand how it is all laid out. Throughout your trip, continue to watch the landscape as it unfolds before you.

THE MAP

The best maps for use in the backcountry are the topographic maps put out by the United States Geological Survey (USGS) and the Canada Map Office. Topographic maps are especially useful because the contour lines indicate variations in elevation. By looking at the contour lines you can tell whether the surface is flat, rolling, or steep.

Where the contour lines are far apart, the terrain is gently rolling or almost flat. You can tell this is so because the contour interval, or the space between the contour lines, is wide. If, for example, the contour interval is twenty feet (the interval is indicated at the bottom of the map), that means there is a twenty-foot difference in elevation between every contour line. Traveling over an area where the contour lines are drawn far apart on the map will be

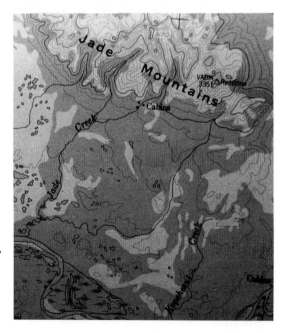

Contour lines close together on a map indicate steep areas, while widely spaced lines mean gentler slopes or nearly level ground.

easy. The terrain will be gentle, and the elevation change may be barely noticeable.

Where the contour lines are bunched tightly together, the terrain is steep. This is because the elevation gains indicated by the contour lines are right next to each other. When traveling over terrain described on the map by closely drawn contour lines, you will not have to go far to experience rapid changes in elevation. An extremely steep pitch, such as a cliff, will be represented on a topographic map by contour lines that are right on top of one another.

The other important thing to know about contour lines is how they indicate the direction water flows. Without this knowledge, you may not know which way to follow a stream out of the mountains or how to use it as a reference point.

The valleys of streams, creeks, and rivers are always indicated by V's, with the apex, or point, of the V pointing upstream. This is because streams are always between ridges or heights of land. Where the contour lines of the ridges on either side of the stream come together they form the letter V. If the valley is broad, the contour lines outlining it may take the shape of a U instead of a V. However, the important point is that the apex always points upstream.

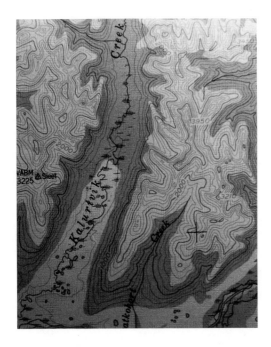

Stream valleys are shaped like V's, with the apex pointing uphill; ridge lines are indicated by V's or U's, which always point downhill.

The contour lines on either side of the stream show the ridges. These are indicated by **U**'s, if the shoulder of the ridge is rounded, or by **V**'s, if the ridge is sharp. The important point to remember here is that the apex of the **U** always points downhill.

Once you understand contour lines, and can make the hills and ridges "pop up" off the sheet as if they were three-dimensional, the next step is to interpret the colors and symbols. Once you can do that, using a map will be virtually the same as viewing the terrain from above, as though you were looking down on it from an airplane.

Though the world in winter is monochromatic compared to summer, and though your "aerial view" as represented by the map will be a summer one, you can easily make the mental adjustment.

Green areas on the map indicate places that are forested or covered with vegetation. Blue, not surprisingly, shows water. White areas are places that are perennially devoid of vegetation. These could be permanent snow fields, glaciers, open rock outcrops, or even paved-over areas, such as parking lots or airfields. Black indicates man-made features, such as buildings, radio towers, or mines. Secondary roads are also black, while highways are red. Trails are denoted by single dashed black lines, jeep trails or logging roads by double black dashed lines.

An important point to remember, especially where old trails, logging roads, and cabins are concerned, is that some features aren't permanent. Logging roads, for example, are notoriously poor reference points because once the timber is cut and hauled away, the roads are sometimes abandoned and they become overgrown. If the map has not been field-checked in a decade or two, the roads may have vanished.

Paying close attention to your surroundings will make you a skilled map reader. Matching the natural features to the features as they appear on the map will soon be as simple as reading a road map. The process of converting three-dimensional natural features into their two-dimensional representations is the same in the woods as it is on the highway. Now instead of looking for the exit, you'll be keeping an eye out for the stream crossing.

By carefully following your progress on the map, matching the terrain around you to the terrain on the map, you will know exactly where you are. You should have no more use for your compass than you have when driving your car. Ninety percent of your traveling will be done this way. But be certain to bring along the compass for the remaining 10 percent.

THE COMPASS

Every winter camper should carry a compass and know how to use it. The best compasses for wilderness navigation are handy, inexpensive little items that consist of a free-floating *magnetic needle* in a clear liquid *rotating housing*; an *orienting arrow* and parallel *north-south lines* engraved within the rotating housing; a clear plastic *base plate*; a *rotating dial* calibrated in one- or two-degree increments; a *direction-of-travel arrow* engraved upon the plastic base plate; and an *index line* at the foot of the direction-of-travel arrow where you read the number of degrees from the rotating dial.

Initially, map and compass work can be complicated. Obtaining a basic compass and a topographic map to practice with before setting out into the wilderness is useful.

The most basic use for a compass is to travel in a straight line toward a destination. For example, if you see a peak off in the distance, point your direction-of-travel arrow at the summit. Then rotate the compass housing until the red end of the magnetic needle

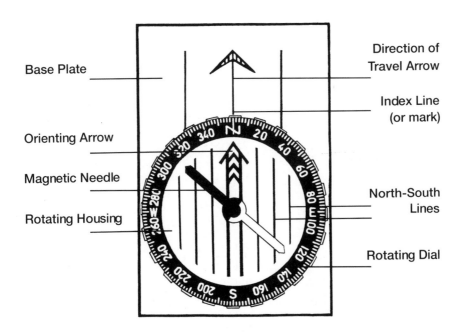

Basic Orienteering Compass. (Brian Wignall illustration)

is floating directly over the orienting arrow. Now, look at the point where the rotating dial lines up with the direction-of-travel arrow and the index line and notice the degree. This is your *magnetic bearing*. You can follow the magnetic bearing directly to the peak by walking straight ahead.

If you travel through areas where you can no longer actually see your destination, a good way to stay on course is to point the direction-of-travel arrow at trees, rocks, or other objects that are on your magnetic bearing-in line with your destination. Also, have your teammates go ahead of you on your magnetic bearing, and sight on them. Then, move up to where they are, and send them out again. In this fashion you can move quickly and easily toward your goal without straying from your magnetic bearing.

The needle of your compass aligns itself with the earth's magnetic field, pointing in the direction of the *Magnetic North Pole*, presently located near Bathurst Island in the Canadian Arctic, some 1,000 miles to the south of the *Geographic North Pole*. The difference between these two North Poles is called *declination*.

Unless you are traveling along the *Agonic Line*—the line of zero declination passing through the center of the continent (running from the True North Pole, skirting the east side of Hudson Bay, and

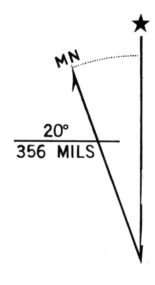

A declination diagram
shows the number of
degrees off True North the
Magnetic North is.
Brian Wignall illustration

cutting through central Ontario, down through Indiana, and western Florida) where the variation between Magnetic North and True North is zero—you will have to account for declination whenever you use your map and compass together. In some places the variation is significant and a failure to account for declination would lead you far astray from your intended course.

In eastern and western parts of the United States, for example, declination reaches twenty degrees. In northern Canada, it can be forty degrees and more. A compass error of only one degree translates into an error of about ninety feet per mile on the ground. If you were to head for a landmark two miles distant in an area where the declination was thirty degrees and failed to account for the variation, you would miss your objective by over a mile!

Since the Agonic Line runs roughly through the center of the continent, it is easy to remember that if you are east of the line, your compass needle will point to the west of True North (declination west). If you are west of the line, your compass will point to the east of True North (declination east). The farther you are away from the line, the greater the declination will be.

There is a diagram showing the declination in the margin of all USGS and Canada Map Office topographic maps. True North is indicated by a diagram at the bottom of the USGS map—it shows a line pointing to the North Star. True North is also indicated by the borders of the map. The east and west borders of the map are lines of longitude. They lie along a True North-South line. Magnetic North is shown as a line with an arrow angling off from the True-North line. The numerical value of the declination is indicated on the diagram.

USING MAP AND COMPASS TOGETHER

From map to field. If you want to follow a compass bearing toward a destination that you cannot see, you will not be able to follow a magnetic bearing, as you did in the earlier example. You will have to take a bearing from your map.

Study the illustration on page 106. Let's say you are in northern Maine, where the declination is about twenty degrees west, and you want to plot a course from where you are (point A) to where you want to go (point B). An easy way to do this is to:

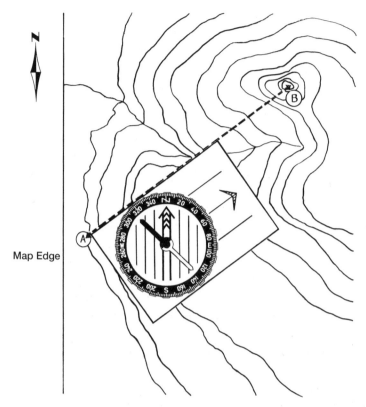

See instructions below for plotting a course from point A to point B. *Brian Wignall illustration*

1. Lie your map flat on the ground (no need to orient it), then locate your position (point A) and your destination (point B).

2. Using the edge of the compass base plate as a ruler, draw a straight line between the two points. Keep the base plate of your compass on the line intersecting points A and B and with the direction of travel arrow pointing toward B.

3. Next (forgetting about the magnetic needle because we are seeking a True North bearing, not a magnetic bearing), turn the rotating compass housing so the N and the engraved orienting arrow point to True North (the top of the map). The orienting arrow and the engraved north-

south lines inside the housing will be parallel to the east and west borders of the map.

4. Now read the bearing at the index line at the foot of the direction-of-travel arrow. This is your True North bearing—that is, the number of degrees off True North that your direction of travel lies. All that remains is to translate this true bearing into a magnetic bearing so you can use your compass to follow it.

5. To compensate for the difference between True North and Magnetic North, you need to add the value of the declination to your true bearing. In this example your declination is twenty degrees to the west of this true bearing, so rotate the calibrated dial counterclockwise until you have added twenty degrees. [If you were *west* of the Agonic Line—say, in Nevada—your magnetic needle would point too far east, so you rotate the calibrated dial clockwise to get a true bearing.]

In the eastern part of the continent, when converting a bearing from map to compass, I remember to *add* because there are more letters in the word "compass" than in the word "map." Other people use little rhymes, such as "Declination east is least (subtract), declination west is best (add)."

Good. You have translated your reading from the map to an actual direction in the field. Pick up the compass, hold it steady at your waist, and turn your body until the magnetic needle aligns itself over the engraved orienting arrow. Your direction-of-travel arrow is now pointing directly toward point B, indicating precisely the way you should go, though you have yet to actually see your destination.

From field to map. You are hiking along a trail in northern Maine, and suddenly you come to a clearing. Off in the distance you see a sharp peak rising above all the others in the range. Just for fun, you take the opportunity to locate your precise location on the trail. Here's what you do.

1. First, hold your compass steady at your waist, and point the direction-of-travel arrow right at the summit of the peak.

2. Next, rotate the compass housing until the orienting arrow is directly underneath the magnetic needle. Then read the

magnetic bearing at the index line at the foot of the direc-tion-of-travel arrow. It reads ninety degrees.

3. But you know that the declination is twenty degrees west and that when you try to transfer this bearing to the map, it will be twenty degrees off. You need to *subtract* twenty degrees when converting this magnetic bearing into a true bearing on the map.

   So, rotate the calibrated dial clockwise to subtract twenty degrees. Now the number opposite the direction-of-travel arrow reads seventy degrees.

4. To locate yourself on the map, place the base plate on the summit of the peak, and turn the compass until the north-south lines on the base of the compass housing are aligned with the north-south borders of the map. Draw a line using the base plate as a ruler from the peak to where it intersects the trail. You are located precisely where that line and the trail intersect.

Again, in the western part of the United States and Canada, the situation is the reverse. Because the declination is east, when you want to transfer the magnetic bearing to the map, you will have to add the declination.

Facility with map and compass requires lots of practice. Most backcountry travelers need to brush up on their skills every time they set out on a trip. The saying "use it or lose it" certainly applies to wilderness navigation.

BUSHWHACKING

Snow has a way of obliterating heavily used footpaths, small rock cairns, and blazes, returning a sense of the primeval to even the most popular summer routes. Every step in fresh snow could be the first.

You don't need to go off trail to escape the crowds and find solitude in winter, but trails don't necessarily go everywhere you want to. Just because someone laid out a trail a long time ago doesn't mean you must stick to it. Some of the best views, deepest gorges, highest waterfalls, and tallest stands of ancient forest are off trail.

Bushwhacking can take you there. To go off trail you need sharp navigational skills and an intense awareness of your surroundings.

Bring maps and compasses, and use them. But also be aware of the sun and its position in the sky. Look around often to get a fix on where you are. Check your progress against distant peaks or ridges frequently. Match these to the terrain featured on your map.

When bushwhacking take several precautions for safety. Wear glasses or goggles in thick brush for eye protection. And keep your thumbs outside of the wrist straps on your ski poles. Pole baskets can get caught on roots or branches as you ski or snowshoe by, pulling you off balance and causing you to take a tumble.

Look out for spruce traps—areas where fallen timber has been covered with snow, hiding the deep holes between the interlacing trunks. Getting through these areas can add new meanings to the word "frustrating."

When searching out the best off-trail route, don't stick to a beeline course. Move around—swing left, then right—and look for the least obstructed, most hassle-free route. Too often novice bushwhackers stick to their compass course and never deviate. As long as you know where you are and where you need to go, give yourself some latitude to maneuver through rough country.

WILDLIFE ENCOUNTERS

One January day while on expedition on northern Maine's frozen west branch of the Penobscot River, I was out ahead of the group breaking trail, unencumbered by a heavy sled for a turn. The foot of fresh snow couldn't slow me down, I felt so light. Skiing along at a good clip, I first heard the ravens croak, then saw them flapping heavily away from me, heading downriver and out of sight.

Rounding a bend, I saw two large eastern coyotes raise their heads, look at me, then bolt across the ice into the spruce and disappear. But there was something left lying on the ice where they had been only a moment before. As I skied the last hundred yards or so, the story of what had happened unfolded as I read the tracks in the snow.

The deer they'd run down was still warm when I reached the place, though the coyotes were making quick work of the remains. It was easy to see where they had cut the deer out of the forest and forced it onto the ice, where through agility, skill, and teamwork they had finally brought it down.

Looking off to where the coyotes had vanished, I could feel their eyes on me, waiting patiently but hungrily for me to move on. I wished them well, then left them to their meal, feeling elated at having witnessed this ancient yet timeless ritual.

Although northern forests are widely considered to be lands that support large wildlife populations, this image is incorrect. It is only because humans have depleted the more bountiful wildlife resources formerly present across most of the continent that this popular misconception persists. In fact, the northern forests are among the poorest of natural environments. Here, animal populations are dispersed because the food sources they exploit are so marginal and so widely distributed. Northern animals need vast uninterrupted areas as habitat, requiring much more range than animals in more benign environments. Further, these animals are only occasionally abundant, being subject to population fluctuations, and they are extremely sensitive to environmental change, habitat loss, and overexploitation. Incompatible human activity such as timber cutting, road building, and housing development can send a population crashing.

That said, winter is perhaps the best time to see wildlife. Animals are more easily spotted in the monochromatic landscape; they tend to stick to well-traveled corridors; and their tracks indicate who they are, how many they are, where they are going, and when they passed by. If you watch for signs and learn their habits, there is a good chance you will see wildlife on your trips.

Through these encounters you can gain a new respect and understanding for animals. When you spend time out in the snow and cold and meet another warm-blooded creature trying to make a living in the winter environment, you realize how closely related you are, how much you share and have in common.

Remember that winter is a critical period for animals because food sources are extremely scarce and as a consequence their energy reserves are very low. Disturbing animals in winter—causing them to run or otherwise expend valuable energy reserves—is harmful and may kill them. If you encounter animals keep your distance, give them plenty of space, and don't alarm them.

As you travel, remember to build in time for enjoyment. If you just put your heads down and push forward doggedly day after day, you may accomplish your mission, but chances are you won't have a lot of fun. Build in time to relax. A day off now and then is a perfect way to rest, take day trips unencumbered by heavy packs, and enjoy your surroundings.

9.
Backcountry
Ski Technique

. . . .

WE SHOULD GET ONE THING STRAIGHT at the outset: you don't have to be an expert skier to enjoy backcountry ski touring and camping, but it helps to be comfortable on skis. You can choose tours that are less difficult and still enjoy a wilderness tour, but to enjoy the whole range of backcountry skiing opportunities takes lots of practice. However, as Steve Barnett, noted backcountry skier and author, suggests, there are skills that are even more important to master: "Good ski technique rates well behind avalanche knowledge, navigational skills, and camping skills as something you need to know ..." in order to enjoy a fun, safe winter ski touring experience.

Winter campers choose skis because they are a versatile, efficient means of transportation. And, while it is true that skis can also be a heck of a lot of fun, it isn't required that you be a backcountry powder hound, sniffing out every delectable back bowl, to become an accomplished ski camper. However, if you should ever want to drop the pack in camp and cut loose, whooping it up in the white stuff, you can do it on skis.

"FREE THE HEEL, FREE THE MIND" is typical mountain tavern graffiti seen in New Hampshire, where backcountry skiing is a way of life. Backcountry skiing is different from the lift-served ski area sport. For one thing, your heels aren't locked down to your skis, so you aren't locked in to one form of skiing. You can go up, down, or across with equal ease. For another, there are no restrictions on where to go. If you want to bank turns through the birches or leave your autograph on a pristine blanket of backcountry powder, it's up to you. There's no out-of-bounds. Of course, there's no tilling and grooming either. What you see is what you get, and the backcountry skier is faced with a kaleidoscope of conditions, from perfect fluff to almost unimaginable crud. You can avoid the tough sections—even take the boards off and walk down what you can't ski. Learning to ski the whole range of conditions takes years of experience. Few have mastered it all.

Backcountry skiing is survival skiing, generally calling for some pretty offbeat technique that you won't learn in ski school. And no matter how beautifully you cut graceful turns when the conditions are right, chances are you'll soon find yourself digging even deeper, right down to the side step, side slip, wedge, herringbone, and the always dignified "emergency dismount"—your basic butt slide.

These tools, often used in rapid-fire succession, will get you down anything you happen to encounter, short of a steep ice climb. But before we worry about going down, let's dig right to the bottom of the bag and pull out the basic stride.

THE BASIC STRIDE

Textbook diagonal striding is the picture of grace. The cross-country racer stretched out in a powerful kick and glide, blurring down the track, is a beautiful sight. Too bad you won't look like that. Wearing a backpack or hauling a sled, striding on heavy boards and wearing your woollies, you're going to look more like a husky than a greyhound.

But don't just plod along. Even though you're not a racer, that doesn't mean you have to walk. Use those skis! Keep up a steady, mile-eating stride. Stay in a secure, comfortable crouch, keep your arms and shoulders low, knees flexed, and swing along.

At first, do a little jog. Spring forward from one ski to the other. When you push off to begin your spring forward, "kick" with one ski and land, or "glide," on the other. Then, repeat, and develop a rhythm. Make a smooth transition as you shift your weight from one ski to the other. Concentrate on moving ahead, minimizing any unnecessary motion, such as bobbing up and down.

The cross-country stride is somewhat foreshortened when you are wearing a pack, but the basic motion is similar to that of in-track skiing. (Maine Woods)

Keep your poles angled back for maximum forward thrust, and make sure they are set out slightly to the side for balance over uneven terrain. Likewise, your feet should be about hip-width apart for increased stability. Make sure to accentuate the weighting of your kicking ski in soft or icy conditions. Finally, keep your head up, and look where you are going. This simple trick will align your weight properly over your skis. Now you are ready to move out!

GOING UP

Straight up. The easiest, most direct way to climb is to go straight up. Just shuffle forward, making sure to look up the hill to center your weight over your wax pocket. Press down on your toes with each step and jog ahead, striding aggressively. Visualize squashing something (you know what you'd like to squash better than I do) underfoot to press down your wax pocket. Angle your poles back and plant them aggressively. Push down on them to provide forward power.

Herringbone. When the terrain becomes too steep, or when your wax gives out, use a herringbone stride. Spread the tips of your

Sometimes it's better to take the boards off and walk up a slope. (Teton Crest, WY)

skis apart and keep them together at the tails, forming a **V** with your skis. Lift one ski, plant it uphill, then move the other. Keep the skis angled as you climb up the fall line (the path a ball would roll down the hill), setting the inside edge of each ski as you place your weight upon it.

The herringbone is tiring and is not a technique for long, sustained uphill pulls. For those, slap on your climbing skins and put it in four-wheel drive.

Traversing uphill. Even with skins on there will be long climbs where you will need to conserve energy by traversing the slope. Instead of going straight up, turn to the side as if you were following switchbacks on a trail. This will allow you to head up the hill at a comfortable angle, gaining elevation that way. When you run out of room on the side of the slope, turn and climb at a gradual angle in the other direction.

Side step. The side step is used to get up short, steep, narrow pitches. Place your skis parallel to each other and perpendicular to the slope. Lift your uphill ski and take a short step up. Transfer all your weight to that ski, then lift your downhill ski until it is alongside the uphill one. Continue in this fashion until you have reached the top of the steep section.

GOING DOWN

Straight run. If you can see the bottom of the slope, the trail looks safe, and you have sufficient run-out room at the bottom, you can just run straight. Flex your knees and ankles, place arms in front as though you were holding a tray, and look straight ahead. This gives you a very stable position, both front to back and side to side. Take a few breaths to relax, shove off, and let 'er rip!

Traverse kick turn. The traverse kick turn is the same as the uphill traverse, only now you are heading downhill. With skis parallel, knees and ankles flexed, and hands in front, start down the slope at a slight angle to the fall line. Keep most of your weight on your downhill ski. To stop, you can either weight the downhill ski, causing it to turn into the slope, or step up the hill (this is called a step turn).

Face the fall line when you descend. (Teton Crest, WY)

When you come to a stop, pick up your downhill ski, turn it in the air, and place it next to your uphill ski. Now your skis are parallel but facing in opposite directions. This is an awkward position, so quickly transfer all your weight to the downhill ski. Lift the uphill ski and turn it so both skis are facing the same direction. Now your skis are parallel and facing the same direction. Continue your traverse.

Side slip. The side slip is a technique to get down a very steep section under control. The position is the same as sidestepping—skis parallel and across the slope. But instead of stepping downhill one ski at a time, roll your ankles and knees outward, or down slope, and let the skis slide downhill on their flat bases. Check your descent by rolling your ankles and knees in, or toward the slope, to set your edges and stop your progress.

Wedge. Sensitive ski instructors have started calling the old-fashioned snowplow the "wedge" to lend it a little dignity. Wedge it is then, and this technique is handy in the backcountry where each run doesn't need to be a virtuoso performance under the lift line. Go ahead and snowplow, who's going to know?

You can use the wedge to run straight ahead at a controlled rate of speed or use it to turn on a downhill when you want to check your speed. Basically the position is the opposite of the herringbone. First, spread your legs. Then, place the tips of your skis together and keep the tails apart, forming a wedge with your skis. Roll your ankles and your knees in, place your weight on your inside edges, and push out with your heels to keep your skis in the wedge position.

To run straight ahead in the wedge, keep your weight evenly distributed on your skis, your hands in front in the tray-holding position. Use the tails of your skis to smooth the snow as you go down the slope. To turn, place your weight on the "outside" ski (the ski pointing in the direction you want to go). Visualize packing the snow under the outside ski with your weight. Push out with your heel and edge the outside ski. Sure enough, a turn will result.

Stem christie turn. The stem christie is an easy turn to master once you have learned the wedge. It is also a lot faster and a lot more fun. Start by traversing the slope with your skis parallel and most of your weight on the downhill ski. When you get ready to turn, spread your skis into the wedge position and transfer your weight to the outside ski. When the wedge turn is almost complete,

Backcountry skiing can involve jumps...(Wind River Range, WY)

trees...(Wind River Range, WY)

lift the inside (formerly the downhill) ski to bring it next to the out-side ski (which is now the downhill ski) and continue your parallel traverse.

Parallel turn. The parallel turn is the natural evolution of the stem christie—it's just a step away, literally! And you don't have to be an alpine skier to do it.

To parallel, think of your legs as shock absorbers, each acting independently of the other. First you sink down on one, then rebound to the other and sink down again. The rebounding motion, shifting your weight back and forth from ski to ski, is what allows you to link turn after turn.

Adding a little speed helps, so start by traversing downhill with your skis parallel and hip-width apart. Be in a flexed-knee position with most of your weight on your downhill ski.

Point your skis closer to the fall line—remember, the way a ball would roll if you let it go directly down the slope. Then, when you have picked up enough speed, be ready to make your turn.

To initiate the parallel turn, plant your downhill pole slightly behind the tip and slightly outside of your downhill ski. Then, rise

or just gentle slopes. (Green Mountains, VT)

up out of your flex, release the pressure from your downhill ski by stepping off, and place your weight upon the uphill ski by stepping onto it. Cross the fall line facing down the slope, and sink into the flexed position again.

The ski you step onto will absorb your weight and carve an arc across the fall line. Upon completion of the turn, you will be traversing the slope in the other direction. Release the pressure on your (new) downhill ski to keep from overturning. Continue traversing until you are ready to turn again.

At high speeds, when you weight and edge the outside ski, the parallel is a very stable turn. But just standing on it is no longer enough—it's a banked turn, so lean into it, as if you were on a bike. Think of standing against the ski instead of on top of it to angle your edges more sharply into the snow—angulation. To do this, your weight must be inside the radius of the turn, not just over the ski. Your speed and gravity forces will do the job if you use your weight and edges properly.

Modern telemark boots and bindings provide a great deal of support, but if you feel unstable with a free heel during parallel turns, really emphasize the flexed position. Accentuate the flex at the knees and ankles so your heels can maintain contact with your skis.

Telemark turn. The telemark is the most beautiful, graceful, flowing ski turn of all. Here's how to do it:

Start by getting into the proper upright skiing position. Place your skis parallel and hip-width apart. Flex your knees and ankles and put your hands out front as though you are holding a tray. Keep your weight centered over your skis, your eyes on the snow ahead.

Now, lower your body by sliding the ski on the outside of the turn slightly forward, the other slightly back, and bending at the knees. Distribute your weight evenly between front and rear. Make sure to press down equally hard on the rear ski, otherwise it will skid, rather than carve, through a turn.

Your feet don't need to be very far apart, especially if you are skiing tough terrain or skiing with a pack. Generally, your rear knee should just about touch your front calf or Achilles' tendon. Although there is no one proper telemark form, it helps to remember that the more upright you are, or the more spread apart your feet are, the less stable you will be. The tougher the terrain, the more stable you need to be.

Now you are in the proper telemark position. Time to ski.

Start in the basic upright skiing position, and head down the hill at a gentle angle to the fall line. As you gain speed and wish to turn, drop into the telemark position: push the tip of your leading (outside) knee in the direction you wish to turn, and press down on the ski with the big toe of your lead foot. This pressures the lead ski, causing it to get up on its inside edge, and initiates the turn. At the same time, press down with the little toe of your rear foot. This puts pressure on the rear ski and causes it to get up on its outside edge as well. Keep your hands low and forward or you'll lose your balance.

Though independent, your skis are acting like one long ski. Hang on and let them do their job. Don't force the turn, but wait for it to happen. It will.

To link telemark turns, drop into the telemark position, push your lead knee in the direction you want to turn while weighting your front big toe and rear little toe, and wait for the turn to happen. Then, after the turn while you still have some speed, come up out of the turn, briefly even out your weight, switch the lead ski, drop into the telemark position, and turn in the other direction. Concentrate on smooth, rhythmic, well-timed ups and downs to weight and unweight your skis. Use your poles to help time your turns as you would in parallel skiing.

Falling. We all do it, it's part of backcountry skiing. Bailing out can be an effective way to check your speed or to just plain stop when your skis feel like they're running away with you. Falling is also great entertainment. Long after the linked turns have been forgotten, the memories of world class crashes are cherished.

Minimize your impact by relaxing. If you feel a fall coming, try to ease yourself into a sitting position off to the side. Then yell loudly so you'll have witnesses to verify your claims to fame.

Skiing with a pack or sled can complicate matters, making it difficult to get up again. When you find yourself buried under a heavy pack in a snowbank, be realistic. There's no way you're getting untangled from that position without shucking your heavy gear. To get up, wiggle out of your equipment, place your skis perpendicular to the fall line, put your gear back on, and resume skiing.

SKIING WITH A PACK OR SLED

Skiing with a pack requires that you de-emphasize many of your skiing motions. The added mass and movement of the pack can contribute to some mighty crashes until you learn to use finesse. Be careful to maintain a flexed, upright posture that is stable and easy on your back muscles. Maintain the carrying-a-tray position and keep the knees bent. This is a strong forward and side-to-side position.

When skiing on the flats or uphill, shorten your stride and move along at a steady pace. If your position is solid you will find skiing with a pack is not all that different from skiing unencumbered. You will go slower and be more tippy because of the higher center of gravity, but the basic technique is the same.

On downhills remember that the results of even slight adjustments to your posture while wearing a pack will be greatly magnified, so make only small, incremental changes until you are accustomed to carrying a load while you ski.

Skiing with a loaded sled is easier than skiing with a heavy backpack. With a sled you don't carry the weight high on your back, so it isn't as critical to de-emphasize your motions. The sled is pulled from your hips, which happens to be at or very near your balance point, so you don't have to worry about restraining your motion to avoid throwing yourself off balance.

As when skiing with a pack, skiing the flats or uphill with a sled requires that you slow down and shorten your stride. Otherwise the motion is the same as skiing unencumbered. On moderate downhills, if the sled has a rigid harness system it will track behind you, so your downhill skiing motion is basically unchanged. As ski patrollers demonstrate daily, skiing with a loaded sled is even possible on steep sections, if you are a very good skier.

A sled is attached at or near your center of gravity, allowing greater stability when skiing the flats.

Skiing with a pack requires balance. (Chugach National Forest, AK)

On super steep downhills where rapid, successive changes of direction are required, the sled is out of its element. The sled will not be able to match your rapid turns, and its weight will force you down the slope faster than you probably intend to go. The solution is to attach a brake rope to the rear of the sled and have someone hold on to the rope to keep it from barrelling out of control. You can also lower the sled down the steep part with the rope.

TOUGH CONDITIONS

In the backcountry you're going to run across the whole range of snow and ice conditions—sometimes in the same day. Here are some tips for skiing less than perfect snow.

Ice. Don't let ice worry you too much. The most important thing to remember when traversing ice is to relax, breath evenly so you don't tense, and use extreme angulation to set your edges. Parallel turns work best here, but if you can't parallel yet, keep the speed way down.

Powder. This is telemark paradise. Let the skis run down the fall line in powder and maintain a rhythm—the deep snow checks your

Proper lift-off will help you ski well in wet, slushy snow.

speed and keeps you from accelerating out of control. Concentrate on weighting your skis equally, and ride that one long telemark ski.

Crud. We're talking your basic mashed potatoes or Sierra cement here—deep, wet slush. Telemarks actually work well in this stuff, cutting a long, stable swath right through it. But because crud is so thick, it tends to stop you short at the end of your turn— it's kind of like having your skis run into a brick wall. If you have too much weight on your front ski, you'll go right over the handlebars.

To avoid the face-plant, keep a lot of pressure on the rear ski, and unweight dramatically at the end of each turn, rising up out of the grip of the thick stuff to change your lead ski. Then, sink down again into a stable position, weight even on both skis, and finish your turn. Double pole planting (planting with both poles at the same time) can help you get the proper lift-off so you can actually do your turn, such as a jump telemark, in the air.

Breakable crust. Not much you can do here. Probably the best technique is to improvise—flailing wildly through a series of step turns, jump telemarks, snowplows, and stem christies. When you get tired of fooling around, resort to the old tried-and-true traverse kick turn, or take the sticks off and walk.

Steep stuff. Face the fall line, even though that is counter-intuitive (in other words, you are scared out of your mind). Keeping your upper body facing down the slope will be terrifying at first, but it is the most stable position for skiing the steeps and puts you in a ready position to anticipate your next turn. When you come out of a turn and begin your traverse while still facing the fall line, you are coiled like a spring, already set to launch into your next turn.

Face the fall line on extremely steep slopes.

SNOWSHOE TECHNIQUE

It's fun to see people approach snowshoeing for the first time. There must be some trick to this, they think. What is it? Where do I sign up for lessons?

I like the way writer Nathaniel Reade describes snowshoeing technique: "Snowshoeing is idiotically simple: You strap the suckers on and you walk. End of story."

Reade is right. On the flats, just walk normally, no need to waddle along like a duck. Newcomers to the sport look like they are doing a John Wayne swagger or imitating a drunken sailor on a pitching ship's deck. There's really no need for the theatrics.

When climbing steep pitches, kick steps with your snowshoes. The trick is to swing your leg so that you flick the tail of the snowshoe up. Then the toe of the shoe can drive flat into the slope. If you are crossing a slope, use the edges of the snowshoes like the edges of your skis and angulate your body, just as you would if you were skiing.

When descending, try sitting on the tails of your snowshoes. Keep your weight back, and scoot down the slopes in a high-speed glissade! Be ready to bail out if you get going too fast.

Use ski poles when snowshoeing just as you would if you were skiing. They offer tremendous advantages when you are striding, climbing, or descending.

One thing to watch out for, however, is *mal de raquette*, or "snowshoe lameness." Mal de raquette is a straining of the tendons that move the toes. It is brought on by the constant flexing of the toes through the boot opening of the snowshoe. Those who have experienced it say the strain works its way into the ankle area, and the only cure is to stay off the raquettes for a while.

"Snowshoeing is idiotically simple. You strap the suckers on and you walk."

CRAMPONS AND ICE AXE

Crampons. For climbing steep, icy pitches or traversing open summits, crampons may be necessary. Those who plan on doing their winter camping in the mountains should bring them along or plan on avoiding these areas. Even skiers and snowshoers will discover that crampons can make traveling in the occasional stretch of tough, icy conditions much easier.

Most crampons used by winter mountaineers have twelve points—ten under the foot and two protruding at the front. The addition of the two front points allows for a technique called "front pointing," or kicking the crampons directly into the snow or ice to form a step or platform to stand upon. The rest of the points are under the ball and heel of the foot.

When using crampons, keep your feet as flat as possible to gain maximum benefit from the points. Some climbers have a tendency to use the inside points when climbing or traversing a steep stretch. Unlike skiing, where edging and angulation work to your benefit, the unfortunate result of this practice is often a fall caused when the points cut away the ice or snow underfoot.

Crampons are either rigid or hinged under the foot. For the winter camper, hinged crampons are the best choice because they can be used with a variety of footwear, from rigid plastic climbing boots to the softer leather backcountry ski boots. Hinged crampons can even be used with mukluks, whereas rigid crampons may only be used with stiff plastic boots. If rigid crampons are used with flexible footwear, the crampons will break.

When you walk with your crampons, be careful not to spear your pant leg or gaiter with your front points. Everyone does it, but be careful. Avoid stepping on climbing ropes if they are in use, and be sure to account for the additional inch and a half or so of clearance you need when stepping over rocks, otherwise you will catch the spikes and go for a tumble.

Ice axe. For all but the most technical routes, ski poles will be perfectly adequate when hiking or climbing with crampons. Even so, if your route plan calls for climbing or traversing steep, icy stretches, an ice axe will come in handy. Most backpacks now come equipped with ice axe loops, so you can carry the axe securely and retrieve it when necessary.

Crampons and ice axes are essential in icy mountain conditions.
(White Mountains, NH)

If you contemplate purchasing and using an ice axe, be careful, because the ice axe can be extremely dangerous if used improperly. Seek out proper training from qualified instructors before using the ice axe in the field.

The safest way to carry an ice axe is to grip it at the balance point halfway down the shaft with the spike pointing forward and the pick pointing down. If the axe is to be used as a cane, grip it by placing your hand over the head, thumb around the adze, fingers curled around the pick, with the pick pointing to the rear.

If you are crossing a dangerous area where you may have to self-arrest—stop your slide down a slope—grip the axe by placing one hand firmly upon the shaft above the spike. The other hand grips the head, with the thumb under the adze and the fingers securely wrapped around the pick.

Position the ice axe shaft diagonally across the chest from shoulder to opposite hip. Stop your slide by driving the pick into the snow using your upper body weight. Press on the shaft with your shoulders and chest. Pulling up on the end of the shaft while pressing upon it with your upper body will put additional pressure on the pick to drive it more securely into the snow.

If you are *not* wearing crampons, keep your legs straight and dig into the snow with your feet to create additional drag. If you are wearing crampons, keep them away from the surface of the snow

The proper way to carry an ice axe: hold it at the balance point, with the spike pointing forward.

Hold the axe in the self-arrest position when crossing a dangerous area.

You can use the axe for added safety on steep slopes.

until you have almost stopped your slide, otherwise they may catch in the snow. Instead, use your knees to dig in and create additional friction.

Whatever position you are in when you begin your slide, always roll toward the pick to minimize the possibility of self-impalement. Never roll toward the spike as it may catch on the snow, dig in, and either be wrested from your hands or spin toward you at a dangerous angle.

Remember, if you fall you will generate a great deal of speed and force. Using sharp objects in these uncontrolled moments is very dangerous. To be able to react properly and instantaneously, before you gather too much speed, takes practice.

10.
Rock and Ice
. . . .

MOUNTAINS ARE ALLURING. The high country is challenging, remote, and mysterious. Mountains are also—relatively speaking—well protected by the laws of the United States and Canada. You have only to look at a map and notice where the crown jewels of our national park systems are located to discover that mountains are a disproportionally well-represented ecological province. Historically there has been less of commercial value in the highest, most forbidding ranges.

The lowlands are not as well protected, but they are even more important ecologically. Wetlands—rivers, lakes, and riparian woodlands—are the wellsprings of biological diversity, home to countless more species than the most spectacular alpine landscapes, and they offer some of the best winter tripping possibilities in North America. Every trip over the ice is a move to reclaim some of this critical habitat from development and exploitation, to give it another measurable value.

ICE TRAVEL

Traveling on an ice-covered river or chain of lakes is a great way to move through the winter wilderness. All across the North, whether for work or pleasure, travel over the frozen waterways was once a common practice. Presently, with roads and trails penetrating all but the wildest country, connecting points with the quickest, most direct route, ice travel is no longer as necessary, but there may not be a better way to cover long distances in winter. On a good day you can go twenty or thirty miles.

Traveling on ice is a pleasure. The wind-packed snow creates a smooth, fast surface, providing easy passage. Animals are aware of the advantage and tend to congregate in the river corridors, where they are easy to spot. The river entices the traveler around each bend. Every wooded point, each rocky headland conceals some new mystery. Upon approach, the scene is revealed like the stage behind a rising curtain. To the Naskapi of Labrador the river is "the immemorial winter road," a way leading to the heart of the wild.

But as with other enticements, there are hazards, and no experienced winter traveler ventures onto the ice without respect and a little fear. Even partial immersion in frigid water can cause at least delay to build a fire, warm up, and dry wet clothing. At worst, the danger can be much more serious. For these reasons it is imperative to approach all ice travel with caution and understand certain characteristics of ice.

Ice-covered rivers offer relatively easy passageways into the wilderness. (Great Whale River, Quebec)

ICE CHARACTERISTICS

Ice that forms during a quick cold snap in late fall or early winter is called "black ice" and when thick enough is a very safe travel surface. The ice is black because it freezes quickly, with no trapped air, slush, or gas. Black ice is strong and supple and will actually sag before breaking. When stressed it sends a spiderweb of cracks running outward from the point of pressure, yet even then may remain intact. Because of this flexibility, it is often possible to retreat to firmer ice before breaking through.

As winter progresses, black ice often incorporates snow into the top few inches and may turn cloudy gray or opaque. If cold temperatures prevail, this "hard ice" may reach a thickness of several feet. Strike it a blow and it will respond with a solid sounding "thump." Hard ice is an excellent travel surface.

Beware of ice after a thaw or "spring ice" generally. This ice, often saturated, has a structure weakened due to repeated temperature changes. Spring ice may be in the process of rotting—becoming saturated and brittle, with a honeycomb-like structure totally lacking in tensile strength. Consequently, it lacks the firmness and strength it possessed earlier in the season and can be quite dangerous. The bottom can fall out without warning, regardless of thickness.

GENERAL GUIDELINES

As a general guideline, an inch of black or hard ice will hold an average-sized person, but two inches are safe. Six inches will hold a moose, eight inches a moose convention. Use your ski poles to tap ahead. The vibrations they send up your arms will tell you about ice thickness, structure, and strength. When traveling on suspect ice carry a hatchet and chip through the ice periodically to check thickness. Always check suspicious-looking ice before moving out onto it.

The keys to safe ice travel are practice, awareness, and not making assumptions. Become aware of the innumerable forms of ice and the factors that affect it. Experiment where you know the water is shallow, where you know you won't get wet if you break through. Study ice before you venture forth on your winter journey.

ICE HAZARDS

Learn the signs indicating danger:

1. If animals deliberately avoid a stretch of ice, you should too. Animals know where the ice is thin, and they will go around.

2. Discolored snow on the surface may indicate the presence of water. If the snow looks dark or slushy, give that area a wide berth.

3. A depression, or slump, in the snow cover in an otherwise uniform surface may indicate soft ice.

4. Keep an eye out for tributary streams, and check your map for them. Their current will keep the ice open in even the coldest temperatures, sometimes for miles. Plan to go to shore wherever a stream, even a small one, enters a river or exits a pond or lake.

5. Ice forming around a boulder or a tree stump may be unsafe. The eddy currents swirling behind these obstructions keep the ice from forming thick layers, resulting in a thin skin with air pockets beneath.

Discolored snow or breaks in the ice indicate unsafe areas. (Maine Woods)

Ice may remain open and unsafe for many miles below large tributaries. (Maine Woods)

6. Rapids, and the outside bends of rivers where the current is moving quickly, are places to be extra careful. The motion of the water may inhibit solid ice from forming. Even underwater springs can swirl the water enough to keep it dangerous.

7. Overflow, which is caused by water seeping up through cracks in the ice or over the edges near the banks, can saturate the snow cover and create a deep, wet slush or form a new layer of ice on top of the old one. If these newly formed ice sheaths are covered with snow, but are not yet solid, you can plunge through them into the wet snow or water beneath—a good reason to tap ahead with a pole.

Your group should spread out when crossing suspect ice. Don't concentrate too much weight in one area. Unbuckle your pack or sled harness so you can shed them quickly if you fall in. Skis and snowshoes are excellent for keeping your weight distributed. You can also carry a ten- or twelve-foot pole or branch to span a break should you fall in. If you are ever in a truly dangerous area where the ice is actually cracking, lie down and crawl away.

Remember that ice is like a live surface. Even ice two and three feet thick will shift with its own weight, water levels, currents, wind, and temperature changes. At first these creaks, groans, and booming sounds will be unnerving, but you will quickly learn to distinguish between ice that is merely shifting and ice that is truly dangerous.

Ice jams, with smashed blocks of ice piled upon one another, form down-stream from rapids. (Maine Woods)

ICE RESCUE

If someone does break through the ice, the whole group needs to act quickly as a team. Procedures should be discussed beforehand, as part of your trip planning, so that everyone is prepared to deal with the situation.

The first step, of course, is to make sure no one else is in imminent danger of crashing through. Look around at each other, make sure everyone is on firm ice. If unsure, people should spread out their weight and crawl to safety.

Next, get a rope to the victim. On ice trips I keep a river rescue throw rope handy for this purpose (though I have yet to need it). If the situation is under control you can tie a loop in the rope (an overhand knot on a bight takes two seconds) before you toss it to the victim so he can sling it over his shoulders. Otherwise, the Styrofoam block and stuff sack that the rope is attached to should provide him with plenty to grip.

Then, span the edge of the hole with skis or saplings. As he tries to climb out, the victim is likely to keep breaking the edge of the hole. The skis or saplings will give him something firm to climb onto. Slide the skis or saplings over the ice, or crawl as far as safely possible and push them toward the victim.

Once he's out of the water, quickly roll the victim in the snow to blot up some of the moisture, then get him out of the wind. Once sheltered from the wind you can get him out of his wet clothes and into dry ones. If you have a large enough group, two people can already be putting up a tent and building a fire. Place the victim in a sleeping bag inside the tent with other people and get a stove (be careful, prime and light outside) going or bring him out in his sleeping bag to warm up by the fire. Keep the hot drinks coming, and make sure someone is with him at all times.

Finally, make sure everyone else is okay. You never know how people are going to react to an emergency. People can become quite frightened once the situation is under control. Now is a good time to pay a lot of attention to each other.

The other common hazard of ice travel is wind. The surfaces of lakes and rivers are open, exposed, and often windswept. The best precaution against windchill is to cover up. Use shell garments, face mask, and goggles to keep the wind from frosting exposed skin.

A word here about ice navigation. On the snowy surfaces of rivers and lakes, navigation is essentially a simple matter of following the route as it unfolds before you. Portage trails and islands can be confusing, but for the most part the shoreline is as good a guide to direction as the shoulder of a highway.

When crossing suspect ice your group should remain spread out. (Maine Woods)

MOUNTAIN TRAVEL

Technical ice and snow climbing are beyond the scope of this book, but winter mountaineering—mountain travel on snowshoes and skis—is not. The range of the winter camper frequently enters the realm of the high peaks. It is here, at and above tree line, that you'll find many of the most spectacular and intensely satisfying winter camping routes.

In the mountains the level of concentration and the skills required can be much higher than in lowland forest or waterways. Navigation is no longer a simple matter of following the shoreline. Wind is constant and blows with greater velocity. Whiteouts—blizzards that obliterate all natural features and guides to direction—are more common. And avalanches are possible wherever there is a slope covered with snow.

But don't turn back now—concentrate on developing sound judgment through experience. Weight your decisions heavily toward safety, and choose simple, rather than complex, routes at first. Gradually increase the level of difficulty as you acquire skills and expand your comfort zone.

MOUNTAIN TRAILS

It happens all the time. You are swinging along the trail, gradually gaining altitude, taking turns breaking out the path, when suddenly you hit a clearing or a stand of mature hardwood forest. Suddenly everyone stops moving.

"What's up?" someone asks from the back of the line.

"Trail's disappeared. It's gone."

"Can't just vanish. It's got to be here somewhere!"

Mountain trails in winter have a way of playing hide-and-seek. Once you get the hang of the game, it can be a lot of fun. Until then it is a source of stress and frustration. I've led Outward Bound groups that panicked when the path hid itself on them. Without the thin line of security represented by the trail, they felt like castaways, marooned in a hostile white wilderness. Perhaps even more, they resented their instructors' cheerful attitude. How could he not share their anxiety?

Breaking trail can be hard work. (Wind River Range, WY)

"Do you know where you are on the map?" I asked.

"Yes."

"Do you know which direction you are headed in'?"

"Yes."

"Can you see how the trail follows this ridge on the map?"

"Yes."

"So what are you worried about?"

You don't need the trail to get from point A to point B. If you know where you are, and know where you are going, you can usually strike out on your own and get there cross-country. The advantage trails offer is that they generally follow the easiest, most expedient route available between the two points. This should be a clue to finding the lost path. Where would you go if you were a trail? Over the cliff or up the avalanche chute? Not likely.

As soon as you lose the path, stop. Retrace your steps to the last known point on your route, and think. There are plenty of clues to find the missing trail; you just have to know what to look for.

The first thing you need to do is think about where you are. Are you on a ridge? Climbing midslope? In a valley? Confirm the terrain, then check your map. Match natural features that surround you to those represented on the map—the brook you just crossed, for

In the mountains extreme conditions can prevail. Even trail signs and familiar markers may become sheathed in rime ice. (White Mountains, NH)

instance, or the fact that you are just below a col. Sure enough, when you look back at the map, you see where the trail crosses a brook before climbing up to a narrow col. You must be right between the two points. No problem.

If there are no prominent features in your vicinity, you can always backtrack to one—an open ridge, a pass, a significant drainage—and locate yourself that way. Go back to your last known point on the trail and start sniffing around. Spread out and look for clues. Look critically at the trees for any unnatural openings or patterns. Often the trail is revealed by a gap through the trunks. Look up at the tree canopy to notice any gaps where you can see big swaths of sky. The trail may be underneath.

Finally, look at the surface of the snow in the direction the trail ought to go. Is there a depression where other skiers or snowshoers may have compacted the snow? Is the snow firm underfoot but soft off to the sides? If so, you are probably on the trail.

Losing the trail happens any number of times on a mountain trip, but the path is usually found within minutes. As long as everyone keeps track of the terrain, finding the trail can be a game, not a cause for panic.

Whiteouts

Whiteouts—heavy, wind-driven snowstorms that obliterate all natural landmarks—are not uncommon in the mountains. One day in February I encountered heavy snow driven by fifty-mile-per-hour winds. It erased the features of the summit ridge in New Hampshire's Presidential Range, a region with such a harsh climate that only tiny plants, grasses, and weather-blasted rock survive. Compounding the problem, my goggles were fogged over. "Damn, it's thick out here," I thought as I stumbled ahead through the white chaos. Just then Joe Lentini leaned over and, fighting the roar of the wind, screamed in my ear:

"You know, it's crazy, but I love this stuff!"

A shadow appeared out of the gloom. A cairn! I tapped it with my ski pole, just to make sure, mumbled a "thank you" under my breath, and felt my way toward the next one.

In this case, even though we couldn't see more than a dozen yards or so, we knew which way we were traveling (south) because the wind, which was blowing furiously from the west, was striking

In a whiteout the team must work together to proceed safely. (Mount Washington, NH)

the right side of our faces, arms, and legs. There was little chance of getting turned around with such an unerring guide, so we concentrated on trying to remain upright and move from cairn to cairn.

At times when even the next cairn cannot be seen, indeed, at times when you can't see your hand in front of your face, you may have to rope up. One person should stand at the cairn while another, attached by a rope, searches for the next one. Progress will be slow, but it will also be sure, and you won't become separated. One hundred twenty feet or so of 8MM perlon rope can come in handy at times like this.

When you can't see and there are no cairns, consider finding a sheltered spot out of the wind, bundle up in your warm clothes, have something to eat, and wait for visibility to improve. If you must continue, make sure to stay together and follow a compass bearing until you get to a safe place. Be careful; even experienced mountaineers have walked off cliffs in whiteouts.

AVALANCHES

Avalanches occur wherever there are snow-covered slopes. Though less common in the wooded hills of the East and Midwest, avalanches are not exclusively an alpine phenomenon. When the conditions are favorable, snow will slide. Every winter camper should have some basic familiarity with avalanches, their causes, and how to avoid them.

In simplest terms, an avalanche is a mass of snow sliding down a slope at anywhere from trotting speed to more than 100 MPH. Along the way, avalanches often pick up riders—brush, boulders, trees, sometimes an unwary wilderness traveler. Anyone who witnesses the awesome power generated by tons of falling snow will not soon forget the spectacle.

Steve Barnett considers avalanches "the single greatest problem facing the ski tourer. Too often you can step into mortal danger without realizing that anything is wrong. In fact, it's often the most alluring slopes and conditions—open bowls full of fresh deep powder, for example—that present the greatest hazards." And it is not just the backcountry skier who is at risk. Hikers, climbers, and snowshoers must also be aware of the danger posed by snow-covered slopes.

There are two basic types of avalanches: loose-snow avalanches, which originate at a single point and fan out, incorporating more

Any sufficiently steep slope can avalanche. (Chugach National Forest, AK)

and more unconsolidated snow as they travel down the slope, and slab avalanches, which occur when a massive block of cohesive snow cracks off a slope and begins to slide.

Loose-snow avalanches often occur during or just after periods of heavy snowfall, when the accumulated weight of the new-fallen snow succumbs to the forces of gravity and slides off. The basic ingredients of a loose-snow avalanche are a slope of twenty-five degrees or greater; snowfall of an inch or more per hour or ten to twelve inches or more total accumulation; and a surface for the snow to slide upon, such as a loose layer of round depth hoar crystals or a snow surface smoothed by freeze, rain, or thaw action.

Slab avalanches occur when well-compacted and cohesive snow layers are not securely anchored to a slope. If there is a weak layer of cohesionless snow, meltwater, or crust beneath the compact layer, the slope is primed to avalanche. All that is needed to release the slab and send it crashing down is a trigger mechanism. A skier or snowshoer may unwittingly provide that mechanism by crossing the release zone, or area at the top of the slide where the fracture occurs, triggering the avalanche.

Traveling in Avalanche Country

The best way to travel in avalanche country is to minimize the risks involved. Be aware of your surroundings; be cautious when crossing danger zones; and be conservative when planning your route or when deciding to ski an inviting slope.

Plan to travel on the ridge tops or in heavily wooded areas as much as possible. Avoid the midslopes or the release zone near the top of the slope. Most victims actually trigger the avalanche that buries them. Avoiding a suspected slope by detouring completely above or below significantly reduces the danger.

As you travel keep an eye on the slopes around you. Look for evidence of sliding—avalanche chutes or slides where the timber has been torn away and open slopes of twenty-five degrees or more, especially lee slopes, which are more apt to be heavily loaded with snow than windward slopes. Look at the slopes around you for signs of snow "sluffs," or small slides indicating the presence of avalanche danger. Finally, keep track of the weather as you proceed. The first twenty-four-hour period after a heavy snowfall, high wind, rain, or thaw is the most dangerous. Waiting a day or more after an avalanche-promoting weather event significantly reduces the danger.

If you must cross a danger zone, gather as much information about the snowpack as possible to determine whether avalanche conditions prevail. One way to do this is to take the basket off your ski pole and probe the snow (poles that join into avalanche probes are a useful tool). If the pole encounters smooth, even resistance, there is less likelihood that the slope will slide. If the pole encounters uneven resistance—if it breaks through crust or punches into loose layers of unconsolidated snow—the slope is clearly unstable and is more likely to avalanche.

A better way to gather information about the snowpack is to dig a test pit in the snow. By exposing a cross section of the snowpack, you can examine the different layers and check for weaknesses. If you see layers of snow characterized by coarse, grainy snow crystals, the slope is probably not safe. If the layers are firm and well bonded, it might be. When digging your pit, choose a safe location on an adjacent slope that is similar in exposure, aspect, and steepness.

If you decide to cross the slope, remove your ski pole straps and undo all pack buckles so you can quickly free yourself from your gear if you need to. Put on additional warm clothing to ward off the chill in case you are trapped; and zip up your parka and fasten all your clothing securely to keep snow from entering through cuffs, collars, or other openings. Use an avalanche cord (a fifty-foot piece of brightly colored 1/8-inch nylon rope that trails behind you and that may float to the surface if you are buried); and make sure your electronic avalanche beacons are turned on, are in good working order, and are securely fastened inside your clothing.

Take a look at the slope you are about to cross. Are there any islands of safety, such as rock outcrops or stands of trees, that you can head to as you cross? If so, plan your route to take advantage of whatever security these natural features have to offer. Head to these islands of safety, or the sides of the slope, as quickly as possible if the snow starts to slide.

Only one person crosses at a time. The others watch from a position where they can see the whole slope. If the person crossing is caught in a slide, the others can locate the position where the victim was last seen. Searching begins immediately below that point.

Avalanche Rescue

As soon as she knows she is caught in a slide, the victim must act quickly to help insure her own survival. There are several steps she can take to rescue herself:

1. When she realizes she is caught in a slide, the victim should yell to alert her companions.

2. She should try to jettison her pack and head quickly to an island of safety. If this is not possible, she should try to stay above the snow by making swimming motions.

3. Before the snow stops moving, the victim should try to make an air pocket by punching out the snow in front of her nose and mouth and should take a deep breath to expand the snow around her chest. The snow will quickly set like concrete, making breathing difficult without this space. She should also try to reach a hand through to the surface above her.

4. If she can, she should try to dig herself out.

As soon as the slope is settled and there are no indications of further avalanching, the other members of the group must take action quickly to rescue the victim. Speed is of the essence: a victim's chances of survival diminish to only 50 percent after the first half hour. What the group does in the next few minutes is critical. Rehearse actions in advance.

1. The rescuers should closely watch the victim's path as she is caught in the slide. They should mark where she was first struck by the avalanche (point A) and where she was last seen (point B) with ski poles, packs, or other highly visible objects.

2. The rescuers should visualize a line between points A and B. This is the path the victim was swept down. A quick search should be made directly below point B. Any clues—hat, gloves, ski pole, etc., should be well marked. If the group is using avalanche beacons, the units should be set to "receive."

3. If the quick search fails to reveal the victim, the rescuers must begin to quickly probe the snow below point B with

ski poles or, better yet, avalanche probes. Standing shoulder to shoulder, the rescuers should advance in a line, probing as deeply as possible.

4. As soon as the victim is located, she must be uncovered. Sturdy shovels are required for this task, and any group traveling in the mountains should bring along two or three. Once uncovered, the victim should be treated for shock, hypothermia, frostbite, fractures, and any other injuries incurred during the slide.

Because head and neck injuries are common, be especially careful when moving avalanche victims.

the professional approach

Vilhjalmur Steffanson adapted native practices and knowledge to explore the frozen regions of the north. *Courtesy Dartmouth College Library*

In 1913, the great American explorer Vilhjalmur Stefansson ventured out onto the drifting arctic pack ice north of the Alaska coast with only minimal supplies. His goal was to explore one of the last great blank spaces on the map; and he wanted to prove that with the proper skills and training, people could survive in what was considered an uninhabitable desert of ice.

Soon after he set out, Stefansson was given up for dead. Search parties were sent, and the rescuers never returned. But Stefansson did. Upon completion of his expedition several years later, a reporter asked him if he had had any "adventures." "Nope," Stefansson replied, "no adventures. Just experiences. Adventure is the result of incompetence."

By using his skills and a few well-chosen tools, Stefansson thrived on local resources where others thought life unsustainable. Stefansson was not just able to endure; he applied himself to the study of his environment—ice, wind, waves, weather, animals—and to the practice of critical travel and survival skills. His diligence paid off: he learned to maximize the benefits and minimize the hardships of his surroundings.

11.
In Camp

· · · · · · · · · · · · · · · · ·

MIDAFTERNOON, and already you feel as though you've put in a long day. Yet there's a lot of work to be done. You glance at the sun to estimate how much daylight remains. Looks like there's about an hour left. To be more precise in your measurement, you take off your glove, extend your arm, and, keeping your four fingers together (not the thumb), you measure the distance from the bottom of the sun to the top of the horizon. There is an even four fingers' width—one hour of direct light, maybe another half hour of twilight. Time to set up camp for the night.

CHOOSING A CAMPSITE

Sometimes ideal campsites are hard to find, but after a hard day, almost anyplace can feel like a room at the Ritz. But if you plan ahead and actually make camping a priority of your winter camping trip, you can spend the night in some fine places. Here are a few qualities to keep an eye out for:

Scenery. After all, you are on this trip to enjoy yourselves, and views are a big part of why you came. Views of surrounding peaks, lakes, or forests add immeasurably to your camping experience. But before you set up your tent, bear in mind:

· · · · · ·

Wind. Be sure your tents won't blow away if the wind starts howling. Campsites on ridges are spectacular, but they are also very exposed. Trees, large rock outcrops, blow-downs, and other features provide shelter. You can judge the wind direction and find shelter on the lee side. Also, be aware that wind can and does blow down dead trees and "widow makers"—trees that are already toppled but are hung up in the branches of other trees, just waiting for a strong wind to send them crashing down. *Always* look *up* when you scout a potential campsite.

Avalanches. Having an avalanche slam into your campsite would certainly be a rude awakening. Be sure to stay away from potential avalanche slopes, and before you set up for the night check to make sure you are far away from any avalanche path.

Cold air drainage. Remember that cold air sinks, so if you camp at the bottom of a valley, your campsite will be much colder than one slightly higher up. Only a few feet in elevation makes an enormous difference.

Exposure. Facing south will give you longer days and more direct sunlight. A north-facing camp will, of course, provide just the opposite.

Water. Having a source of water close by will save lots of time and fuel otherwise spent melting snow. Swift streams often remain unfrozen throughout the winter. If the sources are frozen over, you can usually cut through with a hatchet or an ice axe to reach water. If the water source is frozen solid, remember that melted ice provides more water than snow. Unfortunately, today most wilderness water may contain *Giardia lamdia*, a parasitic protozoan that causes a very unpleasant illness characterized by diarrhea. Therefore, you must remember to purify your water. The best way is to boil it for three to five minutes

Level ground. A level site is always desirable. If the terrain is uncooperative, flatten out the snow to create a level site, or dig tent sites out of the snowpack with your shovels. As we will see, one of the best parts about winter camping is snow—it's a great building material. What you can create out of it is limited only by your imagination.

Hopefully, all your campsites will be sheltered from the wind, be near water, on level ground, with excellent views. Don't count on it, but remember you can almost always locate a good campsite in advance by checking your map. When you get to a promising area,

A well-appointed campsite makes a winter trip comfortable. (Maine Woods)

drop your packs and scout around for the best possible site. When you agree upon a location, it's time to get to work.

SETTING UP CAMP

Once you've decided to set up camp, the group members need to divide the tasks and share the work. At a typical winter tent camp, the tasks that need immediate attention are putting up the tents, building a kitchen area, collecting firewood, and getting water.

Putting up tents. With your skis or snowshoes, pack the entire area of the campsite, especially where the tents will be set up, so the snow is compressed. Doing this hardens the snow, making it easy to walk around the camp area without sinking down into the snow (postholing). If you don't pack the snow, you'll have a hard time moving around the campsite without your snowshoes or skis.

Then, erect the tents and place them with the doors toward the central area where the kitchen is going to be. If there is a strong wind blowing, turn the tents so the doors are at a right angle to the wind.

Tent stakes are basically extra weight in winter, so use your skis, poles, ice axes, or cut wooden stakes. Or, to provide extra stability and security, stake your tent with a "dead man." To make a

Set up a ridgetop campsite against trees or another natural wind shelter. (Wind River Range, WY)

dead man, tie the stake line to a stick, scoop out a hole in the snow, and bury the stick. Compress the snow over the buried stick and allow it to settle. Soon the snow will harden around the dead man like a concrete overcoat.

If, despite your best efforts, the wind continues to tug at your tent, get out your shovels and build a wall around the tent to protect it from the wind. Make the wall as high as you need to. On bitterly cold nights I sometimes mound the tent with snow, creating a hybrid tent/snow house. Have someone inside the tent push the snow away from the tent walls so they don't collapse. Pack the snow so when it hardens, you'll have a wall of extra insulation six inches to a foot thick all the way around the bottom half of your tent, making it extra cozy on even the coldest night.

To add to the comfort of your living quarters, dig a square pit a couple of feet deep in front of your tent for a porch. Having a porch makes it easier to take off your boots in the evening and put them on again in the morning. And you'll appreciate not always having to sit with your legs stretched straight out or crossed.

Finally, when your tent is erect, toss in your sleeping pads and sleeping bags. The bags will air out and regain their fluffiness. As a last touch, hang a candle lantern from the tent ceiling for when you are ready for bed. It's nice to have some light when you get ready for sleep, and a candle lantern will save flashlight batteries

Canvas pyramid-shaped wall tents are essentially set up the same way as the Mountainshelter, only you will need to cut or bring along a sapling for your center pole. Most of the larger, *rectangular wall tents* require the cutting of five small diameter (three to four inches) standing dead spruce poles to use as the frame.

To build the tent frame take four of the poles and erect them as triangles at either end of the tent. Take the fifth pole and lay it across the top, supported between the two triangles. Lash all the poles where they join. Depending upon the type of tent, either drape the tent over this frame or suspend it from the frame. Stake out any guy lines using the methods described above.

Some wall tents come with a valance (a short curtain or piece of canvas attached at the base of the tent walls). The valance is meant to be lain down flat on the ground and covered with snow to provide additional structural strength and support in high winds. Also, it keeps the tent from flapping and prevents spindrift from entering.

Stake down a tent for stability, and make sure the door faces your central fire/kitchen area.

A canvas pyramid tent provides a large shelter in a
relatively simple design. (Northern Quebec)
Photo by Garrett Conover

Erect the stove and settle in. With tent/stove systems, your
work is done. All cooking and living can be done inside the cozy
confines. But if you have a backpacking tent, or prefer to do your
cooking and living outside, by the fire, read on:

Building the kitchen area. The kitchen area is the community
center of a winter camp. While some people set up tents, one or two
others can start building the kitchen area—the place where you
cook, eat, relax, warm up, repair your equipment, and plan the next
day's adventures.

Get the shovels and start digging out a round pit in the snow.
The pit should be at least six feet in diameter for a group of four to
six people, larger for a bigger group. At first, an easy way to outline
the pit is to take a ski, which is roughly six feet long, and measure
from tip to tail on the snow. Another way is to measure a three foot
section of cord and tie it to a ski pole stuck in the snow. With the ski
pole as a center point measure out a circle in the snow. Draw the circumference of the circle, then start digging. After a few trips you'll
be able to dig the proper size pit without measuring.

As you dig from the inside of the circle, pile the snow around
the sides of the pit. When you have excavated a hole two or three
feet deep, there will be a mound of snow all the way around. Pack

this snow with your shovel until it is firm. Then, either carve benches in the snow for people to sit on, or jump into the mounded snow seat first to create perfect, anatomically correct lounge chairs. In half an hour or so these contoured seats will set up and be ready for you to relax and enjoy the evening. Stick snowshoes or skis upright into the snow behind the chairs to serve as backrests.

The rest of the snow around the pit can now be carved into tables, shelves, and counters for the cook to use. If you are using a stove, carve out a windproof place for the stove and storage places for food and utensils. Having the stove, food, and cooking equipment at waist or chest level is a real treat because you don't have to do all the cooking bent over or kneeling down. Make yourself at home.

The fire should go in the center of the pit. The cook will benefit from the warmth, and the rest of the group can bask in the heat, lounge around on the snow benches, and relax. Even on a bitterly cold night, the snow pit reflects an enormous amount of heat. It is only when you get up and move away from the fire that you realize how cold the temperature is.

A traditional canvas tent with a wood stove makes for a warm shelter. (Maine Woods)

Dig a round pit in the center of your campsite for a fire pit and cooking area. (Presidential Range, NH)

Building the fire. Campfires are a topic of controversy—and with good reason. Go to the local state or provincial park and see the blackened areas where the ground is charred and every tree is hacked and stripped. Bits of partially burned foil, beer cans, and half-burned logs are scattered about. Clearly, a lot of people don't know how to make a proper campfire, and the environment suffers from such carelessness.

But to suggest that fires are categorically unsound and environmentally degrading is not true. There is a skill to building a safe, efficient fire that burns hot, doesn't smoke, and leaves no trace to mar the next person's experience. Fire building is like any other winter camping skill—expertise comes with awareness, patient attention to detail, and practice. It can be done.

Care should be used in the selection of firewood, not only to preserve the integrity of the site but to insure the best possible fire. Scout the areas away from your campsite for small diameter (three to four inches) standing or leaning dead trees with hard, dry wood. If you can find one with the bark gone so much the better—it is the moisture trapped in the bark that causes a fire to smoke. Of course, wet wood will smoke too, so make sure your tree is dry.

A tree this size is unlikely to be a residence for birds or small mammals, but check anyway. When you are sure the tree is uninhabited, saw it off at the base right at ground level so the cut won't be noticeable to a sharp eye. Use your hatchet to remove any branches, and gather these for kindling.

Cut the tree into twelve- to fourteen-inch sections with your saw, then split these sections into quarters with your axe. You should have an armful or two of thin, even-length strips of firewood—perfect material for cooking because of the clean, even heat they produce and because you can easily adjust the flame by adding just the right number of sticks to the fire. Good quality firewood prepared in this manner is consumed completely, leaving no partially burned remains and no coals, just a layer of very fine ash.

Before you start your fire, collect all your materials. You will need tinder to start the flame, small kindling to feed it while it grows, and larger wood to burn for cooking, heat, and light.

Tinder can be a strip of birch bark taken from a dead tree or picked up off the ground. I collect dead birch bark and always have a sack full of it for starting fires. Dried grasses, dead pine needles, or very dry, matchstick-thin sticks collected from blow-downs or dead branches also work well. Kindling can be very finely split pencil-thin pieces of your firewood, and, of course, your burning wood comes from the standing dead tree as described on page 158. Place tinder,

Pile the snow you've excavated around the fire pit to increase its depth.

kindling, and firewood in separate piles where they won't be in the way of other camp activity.

Before you begin to build your fire, consider: how will you keep it from melting the snow and sinking out of sight? Also, if you have dug down to ground level, how will you keep the fire from scorching and scarring the forest floor?

The answer to both questions is insulation. If you dig down to the ground, your fire will not sink but it may harm the soil, and you don't want to do that. In both cases a thick platform of dead branches will provide insulation. Find some thick deadwood—rotting logs, old stump wood, or other forest litter—and build a platform in the center of the fire pit.

For added insulation and even more protection for the ground, many winter campers bring small metal trash can lids, metal trays, or cookie sheets to build the fires upon. With these metal sheets placed atop a layer of deadwood, you can collect all the ashes and insulate the ground from the fire, leaving absolutely no sign that a fire was ever built.

Okay, so now you have a fire pit that is about six feet across—wide enough to permit a good draft and provide the fire with plenty of air. You also have bone-dry tinder, kindling, and firewood. Remember, wet wood won't burn, unless you shave it paper thin. And you have a match. You are almost ready. Don't waste a match until you are certain the fire will light.

A well-made and carefully monitored fire need not be an environmental hazard; respect for nature makes the difference between a good fire and a bad one. (White Mountains, NH)

Place your tinder on the platform, and lean a few tiny dry pieces of kindling against it. Now light the tinder. As it springs into flame, slowly feed more kindling onto the fire. Make sure that you leave plenty of air spaces between the sticks of kindling and don't smother the young flame. Let it grow in size and strength, feeding it carefully all the while. Be patient. When the flame has gathered enough strength, start using bigger pieces of kindling until the fire is able to accept your split lengths of firewood. You should now have a hot, bright, smokeless fire—without degrading the environment.

A word about matches—I use the strike-anywhere kind, keep them in waterproof containers, and have them stashed all over the place—in the first aid kit, in my "possibles" sack where I keep all my important odds and ends, and in the pockets of my parka and wind-shell. Bring along a butane lighter if you wish, but remember the butane will not light in extremely cold weather unless you keep it warm. If you do bring a lighter, wear it on a parachute cord necklace under your shirt where it will always stay warm enough to use.

Getting water. Unfortunately, many once pure water supplies are polluted and must now be regarded with suspicion. That we now take unhealthy water supplies for granted speaks volumes on how distant we are from nature and how badly we have abused our planet. Poisoned water is now the norm, not the exception, in all but the most remote wilderness locations. What should you do?

Leave the water filtration system at home—it will quickly freeze into a useless block of ice and plastic. Water purification tablets or iodine drops aren't much use either—their effectiveness is temperature related and they don't work well in cold. The purification method of choice in winter is boiling water for three to five minutes. Bringing the water to a rolling boil will kill all microorganisms.

Getting enough water is much easier if you can get it from a stream or lake. Your map will indicate likely sources of water. If you can find a source of open water you're in luck. If not, cut through the ice with your axe or ice axe until you find it. Some northern travelers who know they will have to cut through two or three feet of ice to get to water every night bring along an ice chisel to expedite the process. When you cut a hole in the ice, be sure to mark it clearly with something visible—a ski, a snowshoe, an evergreen bough—so no one falls in and so you can find it easily in a storm. If the hole is deep, tie a string to your water bottle and lower it down into the hole.

An ice chisel makes getting water easier.

When you melt snow, save a swallow or two from your water bottle and put it in the pot with the snow. The moisture will speed up the process and keep you from scorching your pot. Pack as much snow as you can into the pot, and keep adding it as more and more melts. Keep snow blocks or chunks of ice handy near the stove for melting.

Good work, you've created a typical winter tent camp. It's now dark, and you've been running around keeping busy. But now that the work is done you are starting to cool off. Time to get out of your trail clothes and into nice dry evening wear.

Before you become chilled, take off wet clothes and put on dry ones. Some people change into a soft cotton or synthetic turtleneck (cotton is fine when you are sedentary), dry socks, pile or wool pants, and fiberfill booties. A pair of mukluks over the booties will protect them from moisture, allowing you to wander around the camp area and not worry about getting them wet. Bring your wet clothes over to the fire and set up a drying rack. One of the wonderful things about a campfire is you can dry out your wet items every night. Just don't put any clothes closer to the fire than you can comfortably hold your hand, otherwise you will have some pretty crispy critters real soon.

Now, kick back in your snow-sculpted lounge chair, bask in the hypnotic warmth of the fire, watch the flames leap and dance, and keep the cooks company.

COOKING

You can cook over the fire or on the stoves. To cook over the fire, you need to be able to suspend the pots over the flames. Easy enough: just cut a long pole and stick it deep into the snowbank or the snow next to the fire so it stretches above the flames, and hang your pots from it. Or cut some of your wood into three even lengths about four feet long, lash them together at the top, and use a tripod to hang your pot. Another way is to hammer sharpened sticks (with the hammer side of the axe head) upright in the snow on either side of the fire, then place another stick above the fire and lash it to the upright sticks. Now you can hang your pots directly over the flames. Wire works well, but sash chains (available at hardware stores) with **S** hooks are best. You can use the **S** hooks to raise or lower your pots to regulate the heat. The thin pieces of split wood used for cooking also give you great control over the amount of heat.

Cooking over a stove will never give you as much control as cooking over a fire, but you can learn to make do. Remember to refuel the stove away from the fire and away from where you plan to use it. Store all your stove fuel away from the fire and the cooking area. Never light the stove where you fill it, since any fuel you spill might catch fire.

To keep the stove from sinking, place a metal sheet-such as a cookie sheet, a license plate, or a metal shovel blade-under the stove. Some people use small squares of ensolite under their stoves with success. I always end up with a charred piece of ensolite and a sunken stove, but maybe you'll have more luck. Regardless, you'll need something under the burner to keep it level. And remember, wind is the natural enemy of stove efficiency. Use a windscreen or place snow blocks upwind to shield the stove.

Some stoves (like mine) don't simmer well. To keep from scorching everything you can place a tin can lid over the burner and set the pot on top. The can lid will spread out the flame, creating a diffused, even heat.

Always start with a full tank of fuel. If you run out in the middle of your meal, let the stove cool off before you try to refill it. At the end of the meal, let the stove cool, then refill it so it will be ready to go at a moment's notice.

Start the meal by heating water for hot drinks or soups, and keep them coming. Hot drinks are a great way to replace body fluids lost during the day, and just holding a steaming mug makes people feel warm and cozy.

When everyone has their hot drink, prepare the main meal. The meals described earlier are all of the one-pot variety, so there should be little confusion. Just add the ingredients to the pot of boiling water. Add a tablespoon or two of butter or margarine to everything to help keep you warm while you sleep.

SANITATION

A fresh coat of snow makes the world look brand-new. But in the spring when it melts, the ugliness of poor camping practices is revealed. Half-burned logs and bits of charred sticks are everywhere. Plastic bags and twist ties lie scattered about. Toilet paper and human waste degrade the scene and foul the water supply. And local animals, accustomed to associating humans with food scraps, approach boldly, waiting for a handout. If they don't get one, and especially if they do, they'll chew through your expensive camping equipment to get at your food supply. Another beautiful campsite trashed. A little less wilderness available for people to enjoy.

To avoid creating another such "blackened area," leave each campsite as clean, or cleaner, than you found it. Pack out everything you bring in, down to the last scrap of foil from a ski wax canister. Every time you cook an evening meal you'll have empty plastic bags. Use these to pack out your trash.

To relieve yourself, go some distance from camp (alerting someone in the group that you are "going for a walk"). Be sure to choose a site that is far away from any water source and is well off trail, away from areas of activity.

Some people choose to forgo the use of toilet paper, using natural materials available close to hand. If you choose to use paper be sure to burn it completely or pack it out. Disguise the area and accelerate the decomposition process by covering the waste with rotting stumps, sticks. or other forest detritus.

Food scraps can be burned in a hot fire until they are completely consumed or should be packed out.

Clean up the fireplace by burning your wood completely, pick up your ash-filled lid or metal sheet, and scatter the ashes over a broad area far away from camp, trail, or anywhere anyone is likely to go. Or pack them out, since they weigh almost nothing.

SLEEPING WARM

After dinner, chances are you'll want to relax around the fire for awhile, sipping hot drinks, making popcorn, perhaps telling stories or reliving the highlights of the day. First, though, fill all the water bottles with warm water so there will be plenty for the morning. You can bring these into your sleeping bag with you. The extra warmth will feel good, and they won't freeze overnight. Finally, before you hit the sack, put everything away—stoves, food bags, cups and utensils, you name it. If you don't, and you get a foot of snow overnight, you'll spend the next day digging around for important items. Think ahead.

I don't hang food in winter unless I suspect bear activity. Bears are probably hibernating, and tree limbs and ropes do little to deter agile rodents. However, in late fall, late winter, or during a thaw, bears may be active—and hungry. At these times use your rope and string up the food. An easy way to do this is:

Start with a length of rope, such as your Perlon utility rope:

1. Tie a small, heavy object to one end of the rope:

2. Find two trees approximately twenty feet apart 100 yards downwind from your camp. Throw the weighted end of the rope over a limb of the first tree twenty feet up.

3. Take off the weight and tie off the end of the rope to the trunk of the first tree.

4. Tie the small, heavy object to the other end of the rope. Toss this end over a limb of the second tree twenty feet up.

5. Now, attach your food bags to the center of the rope. A carabiner is useful for this purpose.

6. Haul on the second end of the rope and hoist the food bags into the air. Make sure they are a fifteen feet or more above the surface of the snow. Tie the second end of the rope to the second tree trunk.

7. If you have reason to suspect bears are active, do your cooking where you will hang your food—100 yards or more downwind.

When all the chores are done, sit down, relax, tilt your head back, and look up through the trees at the billions of stars dancing overhead, looking closer than they ever looked before. Perhaps a coyote, or in the far north, a wolf, will begin to sing. Their presence lends a feeling of power and mystery to the winter wilderness.

Before long, a pleasant weariness will overcome you, and you'll start to think about sleep. It is much easier if tent mates get settled one at a time. There is undressing and arranging of clothing, sleeping bags, and sleeping pads to do, and in a cramped tent, getting settled can be awkward. Best to take turns.

Getting a good night's sleep on the winter trail is a real skill. There are several steps you can take to stay warm and comfortable all night long.

Wear plenty of clothes to bed. Forget that nonsense about sleeping warmer with fewer clothes on. The person who said that never spent a thirty-below night in a sleeping bag. The more insulation you have on, the better. Sleep fully dressed, including a hat or balaclava, pile jacket, and Polarguard® booties. If you get too hot, take off a layer.

Remember that you lose most of your heat through your head and neck, so wear a neck warmer, or wrap a sweater around your neck like a shawl. Try to plug any gaps in the insulation around your neck and face, keeping the warm air in and the cold air out. Make sure your nose and mouth are outside the bag—when you breath inside the sleeping bag you exhale moist air, creating a damp, clammy atmosphere. If your nose is getting nipped, put on your face mask.

When you get into your bag, create a small depression in the snow for your hips and buttocks. You will be much more comfortable. Also, remember that you can lose a tremendous amount of heat through conduction to the cold snow beneath your tent, so put any extra clothing underneath you. Make sure your sleeping pads are inflated and positioned correctly. If you roll off them during the night, you'll know it.

Don't get into your sleeping bag cold. Remember, the bag is only insulation, it doesn't generate heat—you do that. If you get into your bag after a quick jog around the camp, running in place, or jumping jacks, you'll warm up your bag much faster.

Keeping some food handy to nibble on during the night provides extra energy to keep you warm. If you wake up cold, eat a handful of gorp or some other high-energy food.

Use the buddy system, and sleep bundled up next to your partners. Borrow some of their body heat—what are friends for?

Nighttime in a winter camp.

If you are still cold after all this, get a new bag before your next trip.

Finally, it happens to everybody. You know-in the middle of the night you suddenly realize you have to relieve yourself. Oh no! "It's cold out there," you say, "forget it!" But then you start getting colder because your body is keeping all that excess fluid warm, and you cannot get back to sleep. Bite the bullet and do it! It only takes a few seconds and sure beats lying awake half the night.

Some winter campers bring a specially designated (and well-marked) bottle into the tent for just this reason. Others use a can, which is more convenient for women (just don't knock it over). Still others have zippered holes in the tent floor-the ultimate convenience.

Pleasant dreams!

SNOW SHELTERS

While tents are generally more convenient, easier to use, and faster to set up, knowing how to build a snow shelter in an emergency can save your life. They can also be a lot of fun to build, and if you are going to make a base camp for a few days, snow shelters can be quite luxurious.

There are advantages to living in snow shelters. For one, they are very warm. On a night when the mercury is shriveled up into a little ball at the bottom of the thermometer (real bragging cold), the temperature will be at or just above freezing inside a snow shelter. For another, when the wind is howling and perhaps tearing down tents (it does happen), inside the snow shelter will be quiet, peaceful, and calm. You will soon forget there is a storm raging outside.

Finally, with a little imagination you can design your own ideal living space—putting shelves here and storage compartments there. And when you light your candle lantern, the ice crystals reflect the light, bouncing it off the domed interior to create a bright, cheerful atmosphere.

If you build a snow shelter, just be sure to put on your waterproof shell garments. You can get wet digging around in all that snow.

Because igloos require a firm slab snow that isn't commonly found outside vast, windswept areas such as the Barrenlands, I'll leave their construction to someone else and discuss two types of snow shelters that are easy to build wherever it snows

Snow caves. The snow cave is perhaps the easiest snow shelter to build—all you need is a minimum of five or six feet of drifted snow and something to dig with. You can use pots, snowshoes, even your hands if you are desperate, but a couple of shovels will make the work go much faster.

Snow collects in deep drifts on the leeward side of fallen trees, boulders, or ridges. The physical obstruction creates an eddy in the air currents, and the snow tends to pile up behind whatever is creating the eddy. So when you are scouting around for a likely snow cave location, start by probing the drifts on leeward slopes. Make certain there is no chance the slope will avalanche before you start to dig. If you aren't sure, move on. Lee slopes along stream banks can be ideal spots for a snow cave.

When you find a likely spot, start digging. Make an entrance about three feet high by three feet wide. Dig straight into the leeward slope, then start angling the entrance tunnel upward. A rising entrance will allow the cold air to sink out of the cave.

When the entrance tunnel is done, start digging out the main chamber. The interior should have a domed ceiling—a shape that is tremendously strong and is most unlikely to collapse. Make the room as big as you like, or, if you are digging in a small drift, as big as you can. Just be sure the roof is at least a foot thick. You can check this as you dig by thrusting a sharp stick upward through the snow. Have someone outside let you know when it sticks out.

Work in tandem with another person who is at the entrance of the snow cave, shoveling away all the snow rubble from the excavation going on inside. When you get going the snow can really start to fly, so take a break now and then, and trade positions. It can be hot and stuffy when you work on the inside.

When you are done with snow removal, poke a hole the size of a small fist through the dome for ventilation. Now you can start working on the interior touches.

Leave your skis or snowshoes at the entrance to the cave, otherwise it will be difficult to locate again in the dark or if it's snowing. Keep a shovel inside in case you have to dig your way out in the morning. And for additional warmth, put your packs in the entrance and block off the door.

The Athapaskan snow house. Building an Athapaskan snow house, or *quin-zhee*, as the Athapaskans call it, is an ingenious way to make a snow cave when there are no deep drifts readily available. To build a quin-zhee all you need is snow and a shovel. You can even build one with just a snowshoe for a shovel. Unlike an igloo, a quin-zhee doesn't require the hard wind-slab snow of tundra regions, and it is much easier to make. The quin-zhee can be built anywhere there is loose snow on the ground.

To build a comfortable two- to three-person quin-zhee, measure a circle about seven feet in diameter. Here again you can use a

Building a quin-zhee snow shelter: after the snow sets up, dig out a living area with a shovel.

ski to outline the circumference, or tie a rope to a planted ski pole and trace the outline. When you have drawn the perimeter of the quin-zhee, start shoveling loose snow into the circle, piling it up until the top of the mound is about six feet or so above the ground.

Let the snow set up for about an hour (depending upon the consistency of the snow this takes more or less time: more for powder, less for heavy snow), then start digging out the living space as though it were a snow cave. Carve out a domed ceiling, punch an air hole, and make the entrance slightly lower than the main chamber to expedite cold air seepage. Block the door with your pack and you are set for the night. Let the storms howl outside! You won't even know it.

Inside the snow shelter you can carve shelves for your personal items or for candles, or customize the interior any way you like. Place a ground sheet (such as your sled wrapper) on the snow, and your sleeping pads on this. Make yourself at home as you would in your tent.

MORNING ON THE WINTER TRAIL

I'm always the first one up, a (bad) habit that only surfaces on camping trips and lies dormant the rest of the year. Maybe it's the fresh air and the anticipation of all the good skiing and snowshoeing to come. Whatever it is, I get stuck with a lot of work nobody else wants to do.

That's all right. Mornings are probably the best part of the day. It's nice to get going slowly in the earliest pale light and watch the frozen world come alive. There's no rush, it's just you and a cold winter morning. It's a peaceful solitude, a communion, that few people are lucky enough to experience.

First thing I do, after checking the thermometer for the overnight low (bragging rights), I get a fire going, put on some hot water, and enjoy the first cup of hot coffee. Too soon, other people start straggling out of the tents, and the business of the day commences.

After everyone has had breakfast, it's time to change into trail clothes, take down the tents, and pack up the camp. Fill your water bottles again, and if you have a trail thermos, mix up some cocoa for a midmorning break.

Morning in camp: quick planning review, then pack up and hit the trail.

If you are switching to ski boots, keep them warm during breakfast by wearing them around your neck under your parka or prop them near (but not too close) to the fire. Put on your boots when they are warm, or you'll spend the rest of the morning with cold feet before they finally warm up.

During breakfast I like to set out my sleeping bag in the sun to air out, and I generally make sure the tent floor (warmed by our body heat all night) doesn't freeze to the snow underneath.

Discussing the plan for the day over breakfast is a good idea. The whole group is gathered, everyone is warm by the fire, and there is time to talk. After breakfast it's time to pack up, load up, and check out.

Check around camp to see that nothing is left behind, and be sure that the camp area is clean. Finally, when everyone is packed and ready to go (and not before), put out the fire and hit the trail.

12.
Cold Injuries
....

WHEREVER YOU GO, at whatever time of year, there are environmental hazards. Beach-goers need to avoid sunburn. Suburban gardeners keep an eye out for poison ivy and ticks. Every place has its dangers, but when they are known and precautions are taken, they can be avoided.

The outdoors in winter has its own perils for the unprepared. Compounding the problem, these situations can be brought on or aggravated by the existence of the more common stresses facing a wilderness traveler—fatigue; dehydration; and the usual assorted knocks, scrapes, and bruises. The winter camper must exhibit an especially high level of awareness and vigilance when it comes to dealing with environmental hazards. The most important are *hypothermia*—the condition of having a lower than normal body temperature—and *frostbite*—the freezing of body tissues. These are medical emergencies occurring when the body is stressed to an excessive degree by the effects of cold weather. Another fairly common winter injury is *snow blindness*—the condition of having sunburned the eyes. Snow blindness happens when the eye absorbs high levels of ultraviolet radiation.

All of these conditions are preventable. However, every winter camper should be familiar with the symptoms and treatment of these cold-weather injuries.

HYPOTHERMIA

Hypothermia occurs when the body loses heat faster than it can be generated. If the loss is not arrested and the situation brought under control, hypothermia can be fatal.

Body heat is produced through eating, drinking warm fluids, and exercise such as walking, running, or even shivering. It can also be acquired from an external source such as the sun, a fire, or another warm body. Body heat is best maintained by carefully monitoring and controlling it like a precious currency—don't spend it all in one place at one time.

Not all body heat loss is a bad thing. Remember the layering principle—to allow excess heat to escape and avoid a perspiration drenching. Uncontrolled heat loss is the enemy to be guarded against. The body loses heat in four ways:

Radiation. A significant amount of body heat can be lost when it is emitted directly into the environment because of a lack of insulation. An uncovered head, for example, radiates an enormous amount of heat that is immediately dissipated and lost.

Conduction. Heat is lost through conduction when you come into direct physical contact with something cold, be it the cold ground, frigid water, or clothing saturated with sweat, rain, or melted snow.

Convection. Your body generates enough heat to keep the layer of air directly next to the skin warm. Your clothing maintains this warm layer by trapping it in the dead air spaces of the fabric. That layer of warm air can quickly be stolen by the wind if proper shell garments are not worn.

Evaporation. When you breathe, you inhale cold air, which is warmed to body temperature, saturated with moisture, then exhaled. This continual replacement of warm, moist air by cold, dry air causes evaporative heat loss. Perspiration also contributes to heat loss because the body must generate considerable heat in order to turn the moisture to vapor and disperse it through evaporation.

Uncontrolled heat loss through any of these mechanisms, or combination of mechanisms, can result in a situation where the amount of heat lost is greater than the amount your body produces, causing hypothermia. Cold, wet, windy days are the times to be especially wary.

Stages of Hypothermia

Humans are truly equatorial animals. We need to maintain a constant temperature of 98.6 degrees Fahrenheit or we become quite uncomfortable. Even a drop of a few degrees impairs our ability to function normally or even survive. A few degrees' drop results in the early stages of hypothermia. A few more degrees, deeper hypothermia. This is what to look for:

Early stages. The early stages of hypothermia (from 98.6 Fahrenheit to about 95.0 Fahrenheit) are characterized by fits of intense shivering and an inability to control muscular coordination. The victim feels cold, tired, and confused.

Middle stages. As hypothermia progresses (from 95.0 Fahrenheit to 90.0 Fahrenheit) the victim continues to shiver violently—the body's way of trying to generate enough warmth to make up for the loss that is occurring. He experiences difficulty in speaking, thinking, and walking. His judgment is impaired, and he may suffer from amnesia and hallucinations. Apathy, even lack of awareness concerning his situation, sets in.

Late middle stages. By now (from 90.0 Fahrenheit to 86.0 Fahrenheit), the victim has stopped shivering and has lost the ability to rewarm himself. He can no longer walk or speak. His muscles are rigid, his skin turns blue (cyanotic), and his pulse and respiration slow perceptibly. He passes into a state of stupor.

Late stages. As the victim continues to cool (from 86.0 Fahrenheit to 78.0 Fahrenheit), he becomes unconscious. He is nonresponsive, and his pulse and respiration may not be noticeable. Below 78.0 Fahrenheit death occurs, usually from a combination of heart and respiratory failure.

Early Detection and Avoidance of Hypothermia

The way to avoid hypothermia is of course through awareness and prevention. Put on proper clothing *before* you get wet, and take it off *before* you overheat and perspire. Protect yourself from the cooling effects of wind, water, and cold surfaces. Be prepared to turn back from your objective, or wait out a storm if necessary. Don't be afraid to change your plan if a dangerous situation arises. Conserve your energy, eat and drink well, and don't push too hard.

Watch for the telltale signs in others—some of us call them the "umbles": stumbles, mumbles, fumbles, grumbles. Anyone exhibiting these behaviors is not well. Stop and deal with the situation before it progresses.

Treatment of Hypothermia

As soon as it becomes apparent that a member of the party is hypothermic, stop and check the rest of the group, for if one person is exhibiting the symptoms, chances are high that others may be in the same condition. Stop traveling and set up camp immediately. As with ice and avalanche rescue, these procedures need to be rehearsed in advance of an actual emergency. Everyone must react quickly and efficiently. Set up the tents, build a fire, light the stoves, and heat the water. Meanwhile, someone remains with the victim at all times and takes charge of the overall situation.

Those in the early stages of hypothermia must have warmth, food, and fluids immediately. Get the victim out of her wet clothes and into dry ones, and into a sleeping bag insulated from the ground. Putting the victim in a sleeping bag with another person can work as a rewarming strategy but only if the nonhypothermic person is wearing light layers of dry clothing. If the rescuer is naked, his or her sweat will continue to chill the victim and may actually prolong the crisis.

If she is in the mid to latter stages of hypothermia, and no longer able to rewarm herself, the rescuers will need to take even more active measures. The victim must be handled very gently in a controlled, protected environment, such as a tent. All possible heat loss must be cut off.

First, insulate her from the cold ground with ensolite pads, extra clothing, pine boughs, or whatever else is at hand. Put chemical heat packs or water bottles filled with warm water (not too hot to the touch) at the neck, groin, and under the arms. You can wrap the heat packs or water bottles in extra layers of long underwear or stuff sacks to keep them from burning or overheating the victim.

Place the victim in a prewarmed sleeping bag. Next, wrap her in a tarp, tent fly, or reflective blanket—whatever waterproof and wind-proof fabric is available—to cut her heat loss through radiation and convection. Let her sip very sweet liquids, such as extra-thick cocoa, liquid Jell-O®, or some other supersweet instant beverage mix if she is conscious. The sugar will help replace energy reserves depleted by long bouts of shivering. However, don't force liquids on an unconscious person.

If the victim lapses into unconsciousness or is lacking in all apparent vital activity, continue treatment and prepare for evacuation. Use extreme gentleness if you need to move her at all. Although undetectable, the heart may be functioning at a very low level, and any rough handling of the victim may cause it to cease altogether. There have been cases of apparently lifeless individuals being successfully resuscitated with no lasting ill effects.

FROSTBITE

I was climbing Mount Adams in New Hampshire's Presidential Range on a stunning midwinter day—the sky was a sharp blue, the slopes a crisp white, and a brilliant sun shone high overhead. But with an air temperature of twenty degrees below zero Fahrenheit and a steady wind blowing at fifty to sixty MPH with gusts even higher, the windchill effect was around 85 degrees below zero.

On a day like this, wind protection is essential, and every inch of my skin was covered—almost. As I turned into the wind to begin the descent, I felt a searing pain, like the sting of a wasp, on my cheek. I turned out of the wind to readjust my face mask and goggles. Too late. A blister the size of my thumbnail was already raised on my cheek where a sliver of skin had been exposed for only a few seconds—plenty of time for the skin to flash-freeze in conditions like these.

Frostbite is the freezing of body tissues and may result in little or no damage to the affected area if it is dealt with early on. Or, if the case is severe and allowed to worsen, frostbite may result in permanent damage or even loss of the affected body parts. The condition is, like hypothermia, completely preventable if winter campers are aware and take the proper precautions.

Symptoms of frostbite can be pallor of the skin caused by a lack of blood reaching the affected area, a sensation of numbness or pain as the tissues begin to freeze, and possibly blistering, as occurred in my case mentioned above. If the frostbite is allowed to progress unchecked, the skin turns white, hard, and eventually the affected area becomes frozen solid.

Frostbite is easily prevented by insulating the body against the mechanisms of heat loss—radiation, convection, conduction, and evaporation. Active prevention of hypothermia will go a long way toward the prevention of frostbite. Remember, too, that metal eyeglass frames may chill and cause frostbite where they make contact with your skin.

When the frostbite is still in the early stages, the affected area can usually be rewarmed by direct contact with another person's warm skin—such as putting feet against another camper's belly, fingers under armpits, or placing a warm hand against a frostbitten cheek.

If the frostbite is more severe, and medical help isn't available, rapid rewarming in warm water is the best treatment. Immerse the frostbitten part in water warmed to approximately 105 degrees Fahrenheit. Before immersion test the temperature with a thermometer. If you don't have one, test the water by dipping your elbow. The water should feel pleasantly warm but not too hot to the touch. Keep the frostbitten part immersed until it has been thoroughly thawed.

Before making the decision to rewarm in the field, be aware that *refreezing* the affected area is very likely to cause even greater damage, so if the conditions that caused the initial freezing persist—inadequate clothing, an inability to protect the frostbitten part—then field rewarming is not a good idea.

Keep in mind also that if the feet are affected, thawing will incapacitate the victim, making it necessary that he be carried out by the rest of the group; whereas walking on frozen feet will most likely result in little or no additional damage to the tissues. Finally, rewarming a deeply frozen area is excruciatingly painful, so it may be best to keep the affected area in a stable condition until medical help is obtained.

SNOW BLINDNESS

March in Colorado—a backcountry skier's paradise. With a foot of new powder and plenty of sunshine, this is as good as it gets. All day we float down the sunny slopes until we finally return to camp, exhausted but happy, anxious to start all over the next day.

Around midnight I wake up feeling like someone is driving thumbtacks into my eyes. The pain is almost unimaginable. Cold compresses help, but the agony persists. Hours later, when medications are applied and my eyes are bandaged, the pain finally abates. Going snow blind is a memorable experience but one I hope never to repeat.

Snow blindness is sunburn of the eyes. As with other forms of sunburn (a surprisingly common winter affliction), snow blindness occurs when your eyes are not adequately protected from the harmful rays of the sun reflecting off the surface of the snow. Snow blindness is completely preventable by wearing dark glasses or goggles with high-quality lenses. Sometimes, as in the mountains of the western United States and Canada, mountaineering glasses with side flaps to prevent excess light from entering may be required.

If you lose your glasses, make a pair of Eskimo goggles. Take a piece of birch bark, cardboard, or wood; give it the shape of a pair of goggles: and cut lengthwise slits to see through. Rub charcoal over the inside of these slits to further reduce the glare assaulting your eyes. Tie the goggles around your head with string.

Treatment of Snow Blindness

Victims of snow blindness will recover in two or three days. In the meantime, if medical help is not available, cold compresses, painkillers, and darkness will help. Plan on making camp for a couple of days until the victim is prepared to travel again.

EVACUATION

Sometimes victims of hypothermia, frostbite, or other injuries suffered in the field need medical attention as soon as possible. After the group has done everything it can to treat the victim and the situation remains critical, the members must decide whether or not to try and evacuate the injured camper or seek outside help.

If the injuries are severe, the group size small, and the terrain complex, the party may deem it wise to send for outside help. In such a situation the group must realize that aid may be a long time in arriving. Some group members may wish to begin evacuation while others go for assistance. At other times, if the victim can't be moved—if he has a neck injury, for example—make him as comfortable as possible, monitor his condition, and await the return of the rescue party.

Sending for help. Two people should go for help. They must travel as swiftly as possible in a safe manner. Safety is paramount over speed—the victim and the ones remaining behind have placed all of their hopes for assistance in the hands of the messengers. They must arrive to deliver the summons.

The messengers should be provided with adequate food, clothing, and equipment but should not be weighed down by extraneous items. They must bring a map precisely identifying the location of the victim and must be able to retrace their route (flagging the route with a roll of blaze orange surveyor's tape can expedite the return journey). Finally, the messengers need to articulate clearly the nature of the problem to the appropriate authorities and make sure that the rescue is set in motion

Self-rescue by the group. If the group can handle the evacuation by themselves, so much the better. Sending for help necessarily means exposing more people to potentially dangerous situations. If that can be avoided everyone benefits.

When the terrain is not complex and the rescue not technically difficult, the group may be better off initiating the rescue themselves rather than waiting for outside help. If the group has been traveling with sleds or toboggans, they are already in good shape to proceed.

All that remains is to bundle the victim (as described earlier—see page 175) and secure him to the sled. Two or three people can then pull the sled with ropes attached to the front. Tie loops in the ropes to go across one shoulder and under the opposite arm for most efficient pulling. The ropes should be of different lengths so the people pulling can march in single file and still take turns breaking trail. A rope should be attached to the rear of the sled to control it on the downhills. Trees can be used to belay the sled down steep slopes under control.

If the injuries are not debilitating but still deserve medical attention, wait until the victim is ready to proceed with his evacuation. A period of rest will do no harm and may refresh him enough to make the trip out with only basic assistance.

Winter campers are also subject to the more common afflictions associated with outdoor living, such as sunburn, gastrointestinal problems, and other complaints. Before you head out the door, take a good basic first aid course, and review some books on backcountry medicine.

13.
Family Camping
· ·

THE SCENE IS A FAMILIAR ONE in the far North. A snowmobile with two adult passengers pulls a komatic, or sled, filled with supplies and camping gear. Nestled in among the supplies, well wrapped against the cold, are the children. An Eskimo family on the move, heading out to the trap line for a week, ten days, perhaps a month. Perhaps longer.

Winter camping with kids? Why not? For the Eskimo family there is nothing revolutionary in the idea. For them, taking the children along on the winter trail is nothing more than working a family business. The wilderness is both workplace and home, winter and summer, and travel is a part of everyday life. It is unthinkable that the children should not accompany their parents. From birth, native children are at home in what European culture calls "wilderness." It is no wonder they feel a stronger emotional and spiritual attachment to "wild" country than do people from other cultures.

The concept of winter living, of being at home in the wild, is an important one for families. It is possible, is in fact still common, to travel as a family and care for children in the winter outdoors. What is not possible is to make lightweight, high-speed, and technically difficult ascents of remote mountain summits and still travel as a family, at least until the kids are older. The theme of lightweight adventure sport versus winter wilderness living has been central throughout this volume. Nowhere is this theme more relevant than in a discussion of family camping.

Why camp with kids? Because if you don't, you either have to leave them with a baby sitter or willing relatives or you have to give up winter camping. There are positive reasons, too. Kids who spend time outdoors from an early age develop a lifelong appreciation for the natural world. From the time they are very young they achieve a sense of peaceful well-being, of centeredness in nature that many urbanized people never feel. A connection to the earth—a sense of belonging—is of untold value in the frenetic and ever-changing world we have inherited and will pass on.

Another reason to take kids along on winter camping trips is the sense of importance they feel in contributing to the goals of the trip. In mainstream society children, especially teenagers, depend upon adults for everything they need and so too often suffer from "the misery of unimportance." It is hard for kids to earn some self-respect, to do something meaningful, to help others, to learn useful skills, to develop a sense of confidence.

On a winter camping trip there are plenty of important tasks to perform, many critical skills to master, and this instills self-respect and a sense of competence in young people. Depending upon their age, kids can help put up tents, build snow shelters, collect firewood, carry little day packs, or help with the cooking. Perhaps now more than ever, family journeys can work to restore the sense of family purpose and unity that existed before life became so complicated.

But before you put Junior in his snowsuit and herd your family out the door, let's acknowledge that camping, winter or summer, isn't for everyone, and there are no compelling reasons why families must camp together. Parents may need a hard-earned vacation from their kids and want to go off by themselves. Kids may look forward to spending the week at Grandma's, being spoiled rotten, and getting a break from Mom and Dad. Also, even if you love camping, your spouse or your children may not. Family unity isn't strengthened when unwilling or reluctant members are forced to participate in an activity they dislike. However, if there is support for the idea, there are no reasons why families can't go winter camping if they want to.

WHEN AND HOW TO START

The Eskimo and Native American way of life takes children into the wild immediately. A healthy child is remarkably tough and adaptable, and if the child is kept warm and dry (just as you would keep yourself warm and dry), there is no reason why a healthy infant can't go with you. As long as they get what they need, they're happy enough to set up shop anywhere—a suite at the Plaza, a tent in the Freeze-Out Range—it's all the same to them. I have seen teeny infants snuggled up in chest harnesses, snoozing peacefully as Dad skied along, unencumbered by the tiny weight, breaking trail for the rest of the gang.

Infants do require some special considerations. Check diapers frequently to make sure the child doesn't have soaking cloth next to the skin. Consider using disposable diapers—truly biodegradable ones, of course—with a lining that will keep a baby's skin drier, and carry an extra waterproof bag to pack out diapers. Change an infant's clothes and diapers in a warm place (inside a shelter is best), and check the child frequently for signs of frostbite or other cold injury. Apply cold-weather skin protective gels to the baby's face and other exposed skin areas. If it is a very bright day, shield the infant's eyes from too much sun. Above all, remember to be vigilant: an infant cannot explain to you what's wrong, and by the time he or she starts crying from discomfort the problem may be more difficult to fix.

To make getting started easier, some families with young children like to team up with other compatible families with young children. Then adults have friends and support and the children have companions their own age. If you choose to do this, remember not to shortcut the planning process as outlined earlier in this book. Just having young children in common doesn't guarantee that your goals for the trip will be the same. Some families will want to push on and cover lots of ground, while other families will want to set up a base camp and explore a smaller area. Families, like individuals, must arrive at an acceptable plan before they take to the woods. Make a base map, divide tasks, gather your equipment, and register your route just as you would if this were an adults-only trip. Refer to chapter one for trip-planning details.

Some nervous parents are reluctant to take their kids winter camping because they are afraid they won't be able to care for them as well in the outdoors as they do at home. Of course they can! The way to do it, of course, is to take home with you and set up shop in a new location. Here again, we're not talking about lightweight, go-fast, do-the-impossible expeditions. We're talking about winter living.

The first step to taking home with you is to view the outdoors as a place where you and your family belong. This takes familiarity, awareness, and a willingness to see yourself as part of nature. If you are not comfortable with the idea of being at home in the wild, stop right now, and don't subject yourself or your family to an environment in which you aren't comfortable.

One way to get comfortable is to try a few day trips first, before you try camping out. Short ski trips together, with the promise of a return home or to a warm lodge in the evening, familiarize children with the winter world and winter travel. They also give you the chance to see how you like being on the trail with the kids. It's something like a planned bail-out on a winter camping trip: you can work your way up to an overnight once you are comfortable with day ski trips. Summer camping trips are also a good training ground. Children who have camped with their parents in summer and been on day skis in winter are much more likely to enjoy themselves when you put it all together for a winter camping trip.

If you can envision yourself and your family being comfortable together in the outdoors, be sure you have your winter skills down before you bring your family with you. You should have camped in winter a few times yourself and be adept at everything covered in this book—able to navigate, travel, deal with emergencies, and set up camp with skill and ease. And you must be reasonably able to handle any situation in any kind of weather. Your children will be looking to you for guidance, instruction, and support.

Finally, when you have your skills down and feel confident in your abilities, bring home with you. The way to do this is to forget about backpacking and use a sled. It's the only way to travel on a family trip.

You can't possibly transport everything you need in winter, plus a child, on your back. This is why you need a sled.

A sturdy sled with a rigid harness system is the answer to the needs of winter camping families, as a canoe is the answer to summer camping families. Not only can the kids ride inside in warmth, safety, and comfort, but you can carry at least twice and up to three times as much weight in a sled as you can in a pack.

Kids travel best by sled. It's an easy and fun way for them to enjoy the journey to your camping spot. (Photo courtesy Mountainsmith)

Look at it this way: an absolutely enormous backpack has a volume of around 7,500 cubic inches. A sled such as the Mountainsmith Expedition has a capacity of 18,000 cubic inches—plenty of room for two kids and gear. If there is still more gear to carry (and you can bring everything you need—diapers, toys, you name it), the other parent can carry a pack or load the overflow in a smaller sled, such as the Mountainsmith Armadillo, with a volume of a mere 12,000 cubic inches. Both of these sleds can be fitted with infant seats (complete with safety harness) and windscreens. These sleds can even be outfitted with dog harnesses, so the entire family can pull their own weight.

Patrick Smith, founder of Mountainsmith, designed these sleds so he could take his two young daughters with him on expeditions in the Colorado Rockies. He recommends bundling the children up in their regular winter outfits, putting them in the sled, and "piling in a whole bunch of blankets. If the weather is cold enough, we put them in their sleeping bags too. That's real cozy."

Patrick continues: "Behind the rear seat go the diapers, water, lunch, and so forth. If it's an overnight trip, camping supplies will go with the kids. If there is too much gear, Sarah Jane will have to pack the rest of it, or, if there's quite a bit left, she'll put it in the small Armadillo sled. We tend to be pretty lavish with the toys and such."

When the kids are older, bring along their skis or snowshoes and pack them in the sled, too. With the sled, they'll always have the option to walk, ski, or ride, and they won't slow you down or wear you out when they get tired.

Sleds are also safer. With a rigid harness you eliminate front-to-back and side-to-side slipping, and they are very resistant to tipping. If the sled has aluminum runners it will track straight behind you and will not slip on a sidling trail. Also, once you get to camp sleds are efficient at hauling firewood; and if need be, sleds are the method of choice for evacuating a sick or injured camper.

A well-made sled with all the options is not cheap, but it will cost less than two large volume backpacks. Plus, as Patrick says, "I look at it this way: figure out how much it costs to pay for a baby sitter for a day out on the trail. It's that simple. Many folks will pay for their sled in one season in baby sitter savings alone. But the bottom line still has to be that your little one(s) will be with you, sharing the outdoors with you and having a great, and safe, time to boot."

TENTS AND STOVES

While not absolutely critical, having a source of heat *inside* your tent makes life a lot cozier for your family. How do you care for your child in the outdoors at thirty below the same way you do at home? Bring a tent and a small wood-burning stove and stash them in your sled.

With a canvas wall tent or similar shelter and a wood-burning stove, you can crank the heat up to sixty-five or seventy degrees on even the coldest night. These tents and stoves range from the very compact and lightweight to the larger, heavier, but more luxurious traditional canvas wall tents and portable, sheet-metal wood-burning trail stoves used by northern travelers and hunting guides in the Rockies. And if you think to bring along a Coleman lantern, you can also have plenty of light to read, play cards, or wash and change the baby. For families (or anyone else, for that matter) there is no need to rely solely on bulky sleeping bags for warmth. In fact, Labrador trappers never even brought sleeping bags with them on their trap line circuits. Instead, they relied completely on wood stoves even when the temperature dropped to fifty below zero. And they stayed warm.

Wall tents with stoves also make every other aspect of family living easier. You can heat big pots of water on the stove for washing children, clothing, and diapers. You can put up a clothesline over the stove to dry your laundry and your wet clothing. And if you choose, you can use the tent as a base camp for exciting day outings or you can move camp whenever you wish. The choice is up to you. Just remember that stoves can become extremely hot. Until the children are old enough, you will probably want to make the area immediately around the stove off-limits by erecting a fireguard or other child-proof barrier

SPECIAL CONSIDERATIONS

Camping with kids isn't all that complicated, and most fears of overprotective parents are either exaggerated or groundless. They won't break. Kids are people too, they're tough, and their needs aren't all that different from your own, so everything that goes for adults goes for kids as well. Kids need to drink a lot, eat well, wear layers, use sunglasses or goggles, and generally do whatever their parents are doing.

However, kids may not be able to tell you that they are too hot, too cold, thirsty, hungry, or exhausted, so parents need to be extra vigilant to recognize their children's needs. The parents are the leaders now, and they must accept the additional burden of responsibility that goes with that role. All the more reason for parents to have solid winter camping and leadership skills before they take their children with them. Here are some points to consider:

Planning. Be flexible. Go through the planning process as outlined in chapter one, but build in more options. Recognize that you won't be able to cover as much ground every day as you could were you traveling only with adults. Even if you pull your children in a sled, don't make every day a forced march. Where four or five miles a day may be fun, six or seven may be a drag. Forget about the odometer, and be willing (and able) to change your plans (see chapter one) if you need to. Also, if you keep travel time to a minimum and set up a base camp, you'll have more flexibility in deciding how to spend the day

Make it fun! Plan on making the experience fun for your kids. Try to look at the trip from their point of view. Imagine what a good time the kids will have building snow caves, sledding, and skiing! The winter outdoors puts any playground or amusement park to shame. Think how entrancing a camp fire will be, how mysterious the sound of a coyote howling.

Make it fun on the way in, too. Remember that long uphill climbs may not be as much fun as easier terrain with lots of fun downhills. And constant instruction from adults can quickly turn a fun outing into an ordeal, so allow kids to learn through self-discovery, experience, and by watching what you do. Instead of formal instruction in skiing and snowshoeing, for example, games such as tag and follow the leader will have them flashing around in no time.

In addition to outside fun such as tag and building snow shelters, bring along some indoor games and books, too. Children love to snuggle inside a warm tent, reading or playing with their favorite toys. If possible, bring waterproof toys, since things will get a little wet. Also, remember to bring lots of extra rechargeable batteries and bulbs for flashlights—children are profligate with them. It's a good idea for each child to have his or her own sturdy flashlight for the trip.

Children love to explore nature. Teaching them about the winter world makes a camping trip a memorable experience.

One more way to make it fun is to keep it slow. Children want to examine things, want to play and rest and move from one thing to another. They aren't as destination-dedicated as adults, and will want to linger on the trail. You will only get frustrated if your schedule doesn't allow for a lot of kid time, both on the trail and in camp. Part of enjoying a winter camping trip with children is to work from their schedule as well as yours

Make it informative. The fastest way to turn kids off to the outdoors is to provide them with secondhand, encyclopedic knowledge about plants, animals, and other features of the natural environment. Memorized information gleaned from textbooks or field guides is stagnant, sterile, and conveys little sense of the intricate relationships in nature. It's like extrapolating an understanding of your automobile from a technical description of a U-joint.

Children are incredibly perceptive and imaginative. They are far more likely to understand how nature works by experiencing it than they are by learning dry facts. To a child a raven is a magical black bird with a most remarkable croaking voice who takes great pleasure in tumbling on the wind, scavenging animal remains, and watching all camp activities with an intense curiosity. How important is it for the child to know that the Latin name for raven is *Corvus corvax*? Does that information add to an understanding of the meaning of the bird?

Let your children do the exploring. Answer their questions if they have any, but don't close the doors for them. Instead, let them rekindle your own sense of wonder, let them help you rediscover your own ability to understand complex relationships with the same sophistication as your children

Rest. Build in plenty of time for rest, especially on a travel day. Plan your travel time for when the kids nap—it will make travel faster. Even if the kids don't need a rest, they may need a chance to run around, poke about, or toss snowballs at each other. Have a handful of gorp and let them play. Join in if you are up to it. Reevaluate your plan for the day at rest stops. If the kids are too tired, unhappy, or otherwise put out, decide whether it makes sense to continue or stop and set up camp early. Constantly monitor the situation as it develops

Equipment. Kids' equipment varies from adult equipment only in size. Kids' skis should be head high or shorter for ease of maneuverability, and they should be waxless for simplicity. High performance is not the issue here. The boot/binding combination described

With just a few special considerations you can outfit youngsters for winter camping.

in chapter six that I recommend for travel over gentle terrain and in deep cold works well for kids.

Clothing. Children wear what their parents wear. Many outdoor clothing manufacturers make a full line of kids' winter clothing—from long underwear to balaclavas—so you can layer your kids the same way you layer yourselves. If they are infants be sure to bring several changes. If you have questions about layering, please refer to chapter 5.

Food. Have the kids plan some menus with you before you go, and make some of their favorites for dinner. Much of what children like fits right into a winter camping diet: macaroni and cheese, peanut butter and jelly, crackers and butter, hot chocolate. High-energy food is very important to a winter camper's comfort, and youngsters, especially picky eaters, may not realize that they will need to eat well. Talk things out ahead of time, and make sure there's enough of what they like to eat to keep them happy

Safety. You teach children about safety in the winter environment the same way you teach them about safety at home, where there are many more dangers—stoves, lawn mowers, automobile traffic, hazardous liquids—for them to blunder into than there are outdoors. When they understand about hot wood stoves (they understand about hot stoves at home), splitting wood, windchill, and ice characteristics, they will treat these things with respect.

Teach them what you know about things like stream crossing the way you teach them to cross a street—by looking carefully before you go. Tell them what to look for. Make it fun. Crossing ice will be just like crossing the street for them, a part of their everyday environment—something they can do safely, intelligently, and without undue concern.

Outdoor tools and activities seem somehow more dangerous than home tools and activities because we are less familiar with them. This is not an accurate way to assess risk. By any measure, driving in an automobile is by far the most dangerous activity most of us will ever engage in, yet because it is so familiar to us, we don't give it a second thought. Familiarize your children to the winter environment, teach them what to look for, what to avoid, and they will be as safe, or safer, as they are at home. Experienced winter campers with children will find that taking their kids with them adds new dimensions to their experience, perhaps rekindling their own sense of wonder and excitement as they share the outdoors with their youngsters. As Patrick Smith says, "I can't really say it's easy—more like it's worth it."

Afterword

NORTH AMERICA'S WILD LANDS and the life and traditions they support are in peril. Every day there is a little less wild country, a little less open space. This precious natural heritage is being consumed at an accelerated rate, and "they just aren't making any more." What is left is all there will ever be.

Wilderness is vulnerable because it is characterized as "empty" and "unoccupied"—a "wasteland." This argument has been used successfully generation after generation by those who don't understand that everything we need and use to survive has a source in nature.

This book is in part a call to action. If wilderness is vulnerable because it is "empty" then let us occupy it. The timeless arts of wilderness travel require wilderness to travel in. When it is gone, there will be no further use for the skills described in this book. Every winter wilderness trip reclaims our heritage, refutes those who argue that wild country has little worth, and demonstrates that the land is already supporting its best and highest use.

So enjoy the wilderness, but also fight to protect the remnants of our wild lands. There is a need for everyone to join in the struggle. Your favorite winter camping destination may be gone next year unless you do something about it. Write letters to newspapers and public figures. Join conservation organizations. Reform your own habits to reduce wasteful use of paper and other wilderness products. Above all, act. It all depends on you.

I look forward to seeing you on the winter trail. Until then, if you have questions or would like to share your knowledge and experiences, please write me care of the publisher and I will respond as quickly as I can.

Appendix A
Other Places to Learn

●●●

IN ADDITION TO LEARNING from this book, learning from other, more experienced winter travelers will help you to develop skills at your own pace in a safe environment. Build a solid base of knowledge you can add to as you gain experience and expand your comfort zone. Following are descriptions of some of the best ways to get started in winter camping.

Outdoor skills schools. There are several outdoor skills schools operating in the United States and Canada, and some of them offer excellent instruction in winter camping. Before you sign up for a course, find out as much as you can about the school: its educational philosophy, the qualifications of the instructional staff, the age and background of the typical student, and the curriculum. Remember that most outdoor schools are tailored to meet the needs of high school and college students, although many are now offering courses for older students, women, and other groups.

The best outdoor skills schools have highly trained, personable instructors and offer a variety of courses. Try to gain a clear understanding of the curriculum and determine if it meets your needs. Read the literature, talk to course graduates, and make an informed decision.

Guided trips. Until about the middle of this century, it was almost unthinkable for even experienced people to head off into the wilderness without a native guide. There was good reason for this practice. The guide was usually a local resident who made his living in the woods and led guests on the side. In an era before precise mapping, it was important to travel with someone who knew the land.

Improved mapping systems and easier access have made the wilderness less remote, and the idea of hiring a guide might seem out-of-date, but there may still be no better way to learn skills than from a good guide. Most guides offer a broad selection of services, ranging from outfitting equipment and providing transportation to leading trips. Some guide services have a schedule of arranged trips you can join, but they may also work with you to design a custom trip. The level of involvement is up to you. Typically, the more you are involved in the planning and organizing of the trip, the more you will learn.

Guide services are everywhere, from the Canadian Arctic to the Maine Woods. There are services that offer dogsled expeditions, ski tours, mountaineering trips, even journeys to the Poles.

As with outdoor schools, learn as much as you can before you sign up for a trip. This may be more difficult because some of the best services are very small and their reputation is word-of-mouth. Ask for personal references, ask about the guides' training, backgrounds, and qualifications.

Outing clubs. There are outing clubs in most parts of the country, particularly in areas near the mountains. These clubs often have an education or excursion department that sponsors workshops and skills training courses. Some of these organizations are quite large and have national reputations; others are local, volunteer groups. Regardless, clubs are an excellent way to get started in winter camping: the people usually represent a broad spectrum of ages, abilities, backgrounds, and interests; the instructors are often well qualified and highly competent members; and the costs can be significantly less than for an outdoor school course or guided trip. An added bonus to a club outing is getting to know the other members and planning future trips together.

Stores and specialty shops. Outdoor stores often organize trips and skills workshops for their customers and other interested parties. These trips, usually to a local or regional destination, are attended by local residents. This is a great way to discover the special attributes of your area and to get to know potential partners for future trips.

Books. Books such as this one can teach you a lot about winter camping. Learning from a how-to book is a three-part process: study, practice, and study some more. Every time you return to a chapter after having tried what it suggests, you will understand the information better.

Appendix B

First Aid Kit

● ●

NO FIRST AID KIT has everything you need to handle every possible medical scenario in the outdoors, but the following list, combined with basic first aid knowledge, is adequate for the most common backcountry afflictions.

Ace bandage

acetaminophen tablets

adhesive tape

alcohol swabs

antacid tablets

antihistamine tablets

antiseptic ointment

antiseptic solution

aspirin tablets

adhesive bandages

butterfly adhesive
    bandages or sterile
    strips

chemical heat packs

gauze pads (4 x 4)

hydrocortisone ointment

ibuprofen tablets

moleskin

personal medications

safety pins

sanitary napkins

scissors

sunscreen

triangular bandage

tweezers

If you are heading into a remote area where medical help is several days away, consult your doctor when putting together your first aid kit.

● ● ● ● ● ● ●

Appendix C

Sources of Information

U.S. Topographical Maps for States West of the Mississippi River

U.S. Geological Survey
Denver Distribution Branch
Federal Center
Denver, CO 80225

U.S. Topographical Maps for States East of the Mississippi River

Appalachian Mountain Club
Pinkham Notch Visitor Center
P.O. Box 298
Gorham, NH 03581
603-466-2721

U.S. Geological Survey
1200 South Eads St.
Arlington, VA 22202

Canadian Topographical Maps

Canada Map Office
615 Booth St.
Ottawa, Ontario K1A OE9

Federal Land Management Agencies

Bureau of Land Management
U.S. Department of the
  Interior
18th and C Streets, N.W.,
Room 1013
Washington, D.C. 20240

United States Forest Service
U.S. Department of
  Agriculture
12th and Independence Streets,
  S.W.
Washington, D.C. 20013

Parks Canada
Ottawa, Ontario
Canada K1A 1G2

Canadian Wildlife Service
Room 1000
9942-108 St.
Edmonton, Alberta T5K 2J5

National Park Service
U.S. Department of the Interior
18th and C Streets, N.W.
Washington, D.C. 20240

About the Author

. . . .

STEPHEN GORMAN is a writer and photographer who contributes to national magazines, including *Outside, Men's Journal, Audubon, Backpacker,* and the Discovery Channel Online. His is a field editor and a columnist for *Sports Afield.*

About the Appalachian Mountain Club

. . . .

BEGIN A NEW ADVENTURE! Join the Appalachian Mountain Club, the oldest and largest outdoor recreation club in the United States. Since 1876, the Appalachian Mountain Club has helped people experience the majesty and solitude of the Northeast outdoors. Our mission is to promote the protection, enjoyment, and wise use of the mountains, rivers, and trails of the Northeast.

Members enjoy discounts on all AMC programs, facilities, and books.

We offer more than 100 workshops on hiking, canoeing, cross-country skiing, biking, and rock climbing as well as guided trips for hikers, canoers, and skiers.

The AMC maintains backcountry huts in the White Mountains of New Hampshire and visitor centers throughout the Northeast, from Maine to New Jersey.

Guides and maps to the mountains, streams, and forests of the Northeast—from Maine to North Carolina—and outdoor skill books from backcountry experts on topics from winter camping to fly fishing. Call 1-800-AMC-HILL to request a complete catalog.

The Appalachian Mountain Club
5 Joy Street
Boston, MA 02108
617-523-0636

Find us on the web at **www.outdoors.org** to order books, make reservations, learn about our workshops, or join the club.

Index

A

Adapting to environment, viii, ix
Amundsen, Roald, 7, 65
Avalanche, beacon and cord, 51, 147-148
Avalanches, 144-146
loose-snow avalanches, 145-146
minimizing risks, 146-147
rescue procedure, 148-149
signs of danger, 146
slab avalanches, 146
triggering, 146

B

Babiche, 77
Backcountry ski technique, 112-132
basic stride, 113-116
going down, 116-123
going up, 114
with a pack or sled, 123-126
in tough conditions, 126-128
Bail-out points, *See* Sheltered areas
Balaclava, 54, 56-57
Base map, 3-5
Bears, 165
Body heat, 173-176 *See also* Hypothermia

C

Camera/lenses/film, 21-22
Campfires *See* Campsite, building the fire
Campsite
cooking, 84-83 *See also* Food and nutrition; Food chart
exposure, 91- 152
features to check, 152
hanging food, 91
morning chores, 170-171
sanitation, 164
setting up camp, 151-170
building the fire, 157-161
building kitchen area, 156-157

Campsite *cont.*
drying clothing, 162 *See also* Clothing
getting water, 152, 161-162
putting up tents, 153-156
settling in at night, 165-167
Canada Map Office, 100, 105
Chemical heat packs, 61
Climbing skins, 74-75
Clothing, 53-63
assessing needs, 54
down parka, 58-59
drying out, 95, 162
fabrics, 55
hand protectors, 61
head coverings, 56-57
insulating layers, 54-56, 95, 166
for kids, 189
for lower body and feet, 59-61
special considerations, 61-62
Summary Checklist— Gear for Wearing, 63
for upper body, 57-59
waterproof shells, 56, 58-59
zippers, 59, 62
Coleman lantern, 185
Compass, 98
declination, 104-105
pre-trip practice, 105-108
using your compass, 103-108
Conover, Garrett, 40, 48
Cooking: *See also* Food and nutrition; Stoves
at campsite, 43-45, 163
Menu Planner, 13
pre-trip checks, 22
utensils, 45-46
Crampons, 51, 77, 129

D

Declination, 104-105
Dehydration, 92

E

Equipment, 24 *See also* Cooking, utensils, 45–46

Equipment *cont.*
axe, 48-49, 129-132
checks on, 22
crucial questions, 25
minimum amount, 52
packs, 26-30
features, 26-28, 30
fit, 28, 30
repair kit, 46–48
saws, 48-49
sleds, 31-34
loading, 32-34
toboggan, 31-33
sleeping bags, 34-40
accessories, 38-40
fills, 34-36
insensible perspiration, 34-35
loft, 34-35
shape, 34-37
size, 37-38
temperature ratings, 38
stoves, 43-45
fuel, 43-45
impact on the environment, 43, 48-49
spare parts, 47
Summary Checklist— Gear for Camping, 52
Summary Checklist— Gear for Travel, 83
tents, 40-43
four season, 42-43
size, 42-43
vehicles, 40
wax kit, 49-50
Equipment Manager, 13
Eskimos, vii, ix
family camping of, 180
Eskimo goggles, 178

F

Face mask, 57
Family camping, 180-190
See also Group camping
clothing, 189 *See also* Clothing, Summary Checklist above
equipment: *See also* Equipment above
batteries and flash lights, 187
skis, 65-69
sleds, 183-185

Family camping *cont.*
    tents and stoves,
        22, 40-45
    food, 189 *See also* Food
        and nutrition with
        infants
    in-tent and outdoor fun,
        181, 187
    outdoor and leadership
        skills, 181
    pre-trip planning, 186-
        190 *See also* Planning
    repair kit, 46-48
    rest, 188
    safety, 189-190
    self-discovery learning,
        188
    time and pace, 188
    utensils, 45-46
    when and how to start,
        182-185
    why camp with kids,
        180-81
Finances, 20-21
    treasurer, 12
Fire-starting kit, 47
First aid kit, 50, 194
Food and nutrition, 84-93
    See also Campsite, cook
        ing food
    amount needed, 13, 85
    extras, 89
    freeze-dried, 9, 88-89
    fresh vs. dry, 87-88
    as fuel, 85-86
    grains, 87-88
    herbs and spices, 89
    hot drinks, 46, 88-89,
        163
    lunch (gorp), 89
    one-pot simplicity, 46,
        89, 164
    packing, 13, 90-91
    water, 92
Food caches, 91-92
    hanging food, 91, 165
Food chart, 93
Footwear, 59-61, 162, 166,
    See also Mukluks; Ski
        boots
Franklin, Sir John, xii
Frostbite, 98, 172, 176-177

G
Gaiters, 59, 60
Gear *See* Equipment
Geographic North Pole, 104
Goggles, 57
Gorp, 89
Group camping, 8-15 *See
    also* Campsite

Group camping *cont.*
    going solo, 14
    group size, 9-10
    job assignments, 11-14
    leaders, 11
    picking a team, 9-11
    self-reliance, 15

H
Hibernating animals, viii, ix
Hooshes, 46
Hunters, x

I
Ice:
    characteristics of, 135
    rescue procedure, 138-
        139
    safety guidelines, 134-
        135
    signs of danger, 136-137
    travel on, 126, 133-134
    wind and, 134, 139
Ice axe, 51, 129-132
    safety tips, 131-132
Injuries due to cold, 172-
        178
    evacuation, 178-179
    frostbite, 149, 172, 176-
        177
    hypothermia, 149, 172-
        176
    treatment, 175-178
    snow blindness, 172,
        177-178
Itinerary, 14

K
Klister, 50, 69
Knee pads, 75

L
Leadership *See* Group
    camping

M
Magnetic North Pole, 104
Maps, 1-7, 98
    making a base map, 3-4
    using topographic maps,
        3, 100-102, 105
Matches, 16-161
Migration, viii, ix
Mountain travel, 140-148
    finding the lost trail, 140,
        142-143
    whiteouts, 140, 143-144
Mountainshelters, 154-155
Mountainsmith sleds, 184
Muir, John, 7
Mukluks, 59, 61, 71-72, 82

Mukluk *cont.*
    with hinged crampons,
        129
    with snowshoes, 72-73
Mummy bags, 35-37

N
Nansen, Fridtjof, 64
Native Americans, vii, x
    family camping and, 182
    skills, xiii
    toboggans, 31-32
Naturalist/Historian, 13
Neoprene, 77
Nordheim, Sondre, 64

P
Packer, Alfred, 84
Pacs, 82
Personal gear, 51-52 *See also*
    Equipment
Personal trip journals, 21
Perspiration, insensible, 34-
        35
Physical fitness, 16
Planning, 1-7 *See also*
    Group camping
    contingency plans, 5
    equipment checks, 22
    final details, 20-23
    gathering information, 1-
        2
    how far and when to
        travel, 4-5
    making a base map, 3-5
    maps, 1-7
    permits and restrictions,
        6-7
    Summary Checklist—
        Planning, 23
    vehicles:
        shuttle, 21
        winterizing, 18-20
Pre-trip checks, 18-22

R
Rae, John, xii, xiii
Rescue: *See also* Injuries due
    to cold
    in avalanche, 148-149
    avoiding need for, 11-12,
        15
    in case of ice, 138-139
    evacuation, 178-179
Rope, 53, 126

S
Safety: *See also* Rescue deci-
    sions on, 11-12
Self-reliance, 14-15
Sheltered areas, 5, 152

Sigg bottles, 45
Ski boots, 69-72
  bindings, 72-73
  mukluks, 71-72
  telemark racing boots,
    70-71
Ski leashes, 75
Ski poles, 73-74
Skills:
  developing, xi-xiii
  in group camping, 11
Skis:
  development of, 64-65
  other ski gear, 74-75
  selecting backcountry
    skis, 65-69
  waxable or waxless, 68-
    69
Sleeping bags, 34-40
Sleeping pads, 39-40
Smith, Patrick, 184, 190
Snow:
  as building material, 153-
    154, 157-157
  mobility and, x
Snow shelters, 50-51, 167-
  170
  Athapaskan snow house,
    169-170
snow caves, 168-169
Snowshoes, 75-82
  bindings, 81-82
  choosing, 77-81
  footwear with, 82
  size, 81

Snowshoes *cont.*
  technique, 128
  webbing, 77
  wood vs. metal, 76-77
Solo camping, 14
Stefansson, Vihjalmur, 150
Steger, Will, 34-35
Stoves, 22, 43-45, *See also*
  Cooking

T
Temperature fluctuations, 4-
  5
Tents, 40-43, 186
  canvas wall tents, 40-41,
    155, 185-186
  Mountainshelter type,
    154-155
  tent stakes, 153
Tillman, H.W., 7
Tinder, 159-161
Travel techniques: *See also*
  Backcountry ski tech-
    nique, 112-132
  adjusting pace, 123
  bushwacking, 108-109
  communication with
    group, 13-14, 95-97
  navigation with map and
    compass, 98-108
  preventing injuries, 109,
    131-132
  Summary Checklist—
    Traveling, 83

thermo-regulation, 95 *See
  also* Clothing, insulating
  layers
topographic maps, 3, 100-
  102, 105, 195
  reading contour lines,
    100-102

U
United States Geological
  Survey (USGS) maps,
  100-105

V
Vehicle, shuttle, 21
Vehicle,winterizing, 18-20

W
Water:
  drinking, 92
  purifying, 152
Weather forecast, checking,
  22
Whiteouts, 140, 143-144
Wildlife encounters, 109-
  111
Windchill, 98, 176, 139
Winter camping: joys of, vi-
  vii